Praise for *House by the S[...]*

MW01257136

"Mrs. L.A. Abbott
testament to that. Mrs. Abbott, through her stories, tells us of an era
that needs to be remembered."

Orville Goodenough, Morrison Historical Society

"Born within living memory of the Civil War, my
grandmother, with a perceptive eye, became the Boswell of rural life.
Her stories are a vivid education into the exotic, immediate past when
hobos traveling the Lincoln Highway made annual visits to congenial
homes, horses were harnessed for daily labor and cotton candy at the
county fair was the supreme treat of summer for a farm boy."

Chuck Abbott, Commodities Correspondent
Reuters, Washington D.C.

"*House by the Side of the Road* is a treasure, a slim and lovely
volume of stories of the everyday tales, history and musings about
'The Good Old Days' we've all heard before but didn't have the good
sense or literary skill to write 'em down. Mrs. Abbott did and through
them we learn about the promise and peril of 20th century farm life.
More importantly, we meet Illinois' early settlers, the yeoman farmers
and the good and decent (and some less decent) people that moved up
and down the highway of her life—and now, into ours. *House by the
Side of the Road* is a keeper, to be read and read again. Its stories are
ageless and its simple, clear message is priceless. Thank you for
writing 'em down, Mrs. Abbott, thank you."

Alan Guebert, Columnist
The Farm and Food File

"These stories should resonate all along the great Lincoln
Highway, and beyond. At one level, Mrs. Abbott's sharp eye, keen wit
and great story-telling style provide an interesting, first-hand view of
farm life during a dynamic half century. Beyond that, as one who has
lived at five spots along the Highway, from Cheyenne to Chicago
Heights, I say 'Amen' to the Lincoln Highway spirit and the boundless
hospitality reflected in *House by the Side of the Road*."

Jim Evans, Professor of Agricultural Communications (retired)
University of Illinois, Urbana-Champaign

HOUSE

BY THE SIDE OF THE

ROAD

*Stories of 20th Century farm life
beside Illinois' Lincoln Highway*

by

Mrs. L. A. Abbott

PINES PUBLISHING, INC.

MORRISON, ILLINOIS

WWW.PINESPUBLISHING.COM

Library of Congress Control Number: 2005902509

ISBN 0-9766820-0-1

First Printing June 2005

Printed in the United States by Morris Publishing
3212 East Highway 30
Kearney, NE 68847
1-800-650-7888

Table of Contents

Young farm boy Orville Goodenough, age 7, holding Dan and Prince, fresh from the field with another 36 bushels of hand-picked corn for the crib, during the 1937 harvest. He leans against the bangboards, used to bounce overthrown ears back into the wagon. (Courtesy of Orville Goodenough)

Foreword

I have had the opportunity over the past few years to be involved with the Morrison Historical Society and its Heritage Museum. It is a relatively small museum, but has thousands of items in its inventory. They range all the way from a small Bible that was found in the home of the family killed in the Ottawa Indian Massacre of 1832, to a piece of concrete that was part of the original Lincoln Highway, the road that runs past the "house by the side of the road." All these thousands of items have one thing in common. They all have a story behind them.

One of our many human faults is that we seldom put our actions and thoughts down in writing and so our stories are lost. There are so many items at the Museum that may have some small reference, but little else. We have to try and research more information. Sometimes we are successful, sometimes not, and in those cases the story is lost.

Mrs. L.A. Abbott was a story teller, and this book is a testament to that. She was a frequent participant in community activities and she reported on these. More importantly, she wrote about the "little things," and that is what this book is about. Times change—we wouldn't have it any other way—but we need to remember what used to be. Mrs. Abbott, through her stories, tells us of an era that needs to be remembered.

If you are older, then you can relate to many of these stories, or recall your parents telling you about them. If you are young, it is an opportunity to feel a bit of your heritage and to connect with this community. Perhaps it will make you start writing down your own stories, because sometime in the future, others will want to know the story of your "era."

So THANK YOU, Mrs. Abbott, for sharing your stories. Your words allow all of us to be able to relive a little bit of what life used to be like at the House by the Side of the Road!

Orville Goodenough
Morrison, Illinois
March 11, 2005

This cross-stitch sampler was a gift to the bride from her new mother-in-law, Sarah G. Abbott, in 1923. The author took the words to heart, and it held a place of honor in her home.

Preface

Mrs. L.A. Abbott lived in the House by the Side of the Road for 66 years, from the day she married our grandfather in 1923 until the day she died in 1989. A hard-working farm wife, Grandma was the front line in watching over the homestead whether she was looking out the kitchen window, hanging laundry on the clothesline or gardening, her favorite activity.

Active, observant and always willing to help, Grandma met a variety of interesting people who happened along the Road—U.S. Route 30, also known as the Lincoln Highway. These are her stories of some of those many and varied encounters in the age before interstate highways, reliable cars and cell phones.

The House by the Side of the Road originally was built in 1848, when our great-great-grandfather, Asa M. Abbott, settled in Whiteside County, Illinois. The Road then wasn't much more than a wagon trail that connected Ft. Dearborn (Chicago) with the "narrows" of the Mississippi River at Fulton. A gunsmith, Asa knew his business depended on being visible from the trail, so he built his home within 50 yards of the Road. Although the original house was replaced with the current structure in 1955, the location remains the same—close to the Road.

When a farm's front yard is as close to the Road as if you lived on a street in town, visibility is a given. Add a second house to the property, as occurred shortly after our grandparents married, and you become the most favorable option for travelers who need help: Double the number of houses served by one driveway means double the chance of finding someone home.

And, in the days when farm families made a trip to town not more than weekly, it was pretty likely that there would be someone home. That someone was our grandmother, who referred to herself as Mrs. L.A. Abbott far more than she referred to herself as Eunice Abbott—because that's just the way it was done in her generation.

In the evening, after the day's work was done and the supper dishes had been washed, dried and put away, Grandma focused on creative pastimes. Many of her farm-wife friends did handiwork, such as embroidery, knitting or quilting in those evening hours. Not Grandma. For her, it was reading and writing. The stories in this book are a result of the countless evenings Grandma spent in front of her manual Olympia typewriter—often until the wee hours, as evidenced by the light coming from her window that we could see from our house across the driveway.

These are real-life stories of farm life along the busy Lincoln Highway from the 1920s through the 1980s. They take you back to a time when being neighborly meant opening your home to those in need—even if they were strangers. Grandma wrote about those who knocked on the door because they needed a gallon of gas or a tow to the nearest mechanic. Strangers working their way across the country in the Great Depression, willing to pick apples or strawberries in exchange for a place to camp out, their daily meals and a few dollars. Piano salesmen who knew that a thunderstorm would help them get a piano inside a farm house quickly. Hobos who chopped wood in exchange for a homemade supper. A bicycle rider who asked unusual questions and made residents of the House by the Side of the Road wonder if he were a spy trying to find the assassin of Martin Luther King Jr.

To Grandma and those of her generation, "farm wife" was a full-time job with tremendous responsibility. While the "men-folk" tended to the crops and livestock from dawn until dusk, farm wives kept the family (and the hired hands) fed, supplied with clean clothes and a warm, inviting home. Before the advent of automatic washing machines and at a time when producing and preserving food took more than a trip to the store, it was a 24/7 job decades before that phrase took hold. Grandma wrote about everyday life on the family farm, including what apparently was not one of her favorite "extra duties"— picking corn. She also chronicles the stories passed down verbally for generations about the big, red barn and its role as a stop on the Underground Railroad in the 1850s.

Besides stories about rural life on the Abbott farm along the Lincoln Highway, Grandma also had a passion for two other topics— country schools and the Whiteside County Fair. Grandma taught at the Crouch School, a one-room school just a couple of miles from the House by the Side of the Road, before she married in the 1920s. Through her stories, she has recorded school-year highlights of these

Preface

long-gone places, which served the social purpose of bringing rural neighbors together in celebration of life and their agricultural heritage.

As long-time superintendent of the Ag Products, Horticulture and Floriculture Departments at the Whiteside County Fair, celebrating its 135th edition in Morrison's Sesquicentennial year of 2005, Grandma also took it upon herself to become Fair historian. She tells of a time when coming to the Fair was an extra-special outing demanding the finest of clothing and a picnic lunch on a white linen tablecloth underneath the big, shady oak trees. When one, thin dime could provide a day's worth of entertainment to a small child—including a ride on the merry-go-round. When the old, wooden original structures on the fairgrounds were replaced by shiny, new, secure buildings to show off everything from sheep to vegetables to cakes and hobbies. And, she recounts the stories of the cabins built on the fairgrounds by the "Old Settlers," the original families of Whiteside County.

House by the Side of the Road gives us all a peek into rural life throughout the early to mid-20th century. A time when the family farm was self-sustaining, horses were the ones providing horse power and getting the crops in before Thanksgiving was a milestone to be rewarded with a rabbit hunt on Turkey Day. When everyone was struggling to survive the Great Depression. When rural neighbors congregated at the local one-room school for Christmas pageants and the annual Corn Carnival. When residents of the House by the Side of the Road opened their hearts and home to the strangers who knocked on the door.

Susan Abbott Gidel
Jan Abbott Landow
March 2005

Author Biography & Acknowledgements

Mrs. L.A. Abbott was born in Clinton, Iowa in 1898, but lived nearly all her life across the Mississippi River in Whiteside County, Illinois. Eunice Pingel grew up in Fulton, Ill., taught in a one-room school halfway between Fulton and Morrison, Ill., and married L.A. Abbott in June 1923, moving to his family farm six miles west of Morrison where she lived the rest of her days. She raised two sons, William Morton and Edward Theodore, countless generations of farm cats, scores of vegetable gardens and thousands of peonies, hydrangea and lilacs. During her "spare time," she was a local correspondent for three newspapers, reporting the births, deaths, comings and goings of her rural neighborhood, Cottonwood. She died in July 1989 at the age of 92.

Susan Abbott Gidel and Jan Abbott Landow are granddaughters of the author, growing up across the driveway from Grandma and the House by the Side of the Road. We both attribute our professional accomplishments as a writer and photographer, respectively, to the early influence of our grandmother. Also, we both thank Grandma for being an original believer in "save everything because you never know when you might need it again." This book would not have been possible without her conscientious effort to save her manuscripts and keep them all in one place. Thanks, Grandma.

We'd like to especially thank Orville Goodenough, a long-time family friend and local historian, for providing a heartfelt introduction to this collection as well as a reminder to us all about the importance of personal story-telling.

Thanks, too, to Brett Landow and Jerry Gidel, husbands who understood why this project was important and provided unending support. Also, to Sara Ramach for advice and a keen editor's eye.

Finally, thanks to Ed and Dorothy Abbott, the fifth generation to reside in the House by the Side of the Road, for maintaining the traditions and life at The Pines until the sixth generation is ready to move back home.

Mr. and Mrs. L.A. Abbott, flanked by sons Edward (left) and William, in 1942. That's a 1938 Ford behind them.

1. The Big Red Barn

Written circa 1985

The big, old, red barn on the north side of U.S. 30, now called Lincoln Road, in Whiteside County, Ill., looks about the same from the road as it did nearly 130 years ago. But look closely; there have been a few changes to the exterior and many changes inside, according to stories of the Good Old Days—changes that have come one by one as farming methods changed.

L.A. Abbott clears snow in front of the corncrib and the big red barn.

The farm has been in the Abbott family since patent to Benjamin Abbott, on July 27, 1848. He was the fifth generation from George Abbott, who came to America in 1637. Perhaps the continued

The Big Red Barn

interest in Hereford cattle relates to George who was born in Hertfordshire, England, in 1615.

Originally the barn was a rectangular building about 60 by 30 feet, but as conditions changed, several additions were made. Fifteen feet were added along all the north side to accommodate cattle, which increased the hay storage capacity also. Another fifteen-foot addition on the southeast corner of the barn made room for a stairway to the haymow above the grain bins. They were in the center of the building, east of the driveway that would accommodate loads of grain or hay. Big metal doors have replaced the original wooden doors.

In those early days, horses were a necessity and valuable, deserving the warmest quarters in cold weather. Cattle were important, too, but usually got second choice. As the barn was designed, there were four double stalls and two single stalls for the horses along the east side, box stalls, with heavy wooden pegs on the wall behind to hang each horse's harness. Along the colder, north, side of the barn were five double box stalls and five stanchions for cattle, with gutter for cleaning and an exit door to the west. In the original plan, the entire west side of the barn, from floor to roof was for hay, a good insulation from the cold winds. Loose hay took lots of space, as baled forage hadn't been "invented" yet.

The barn was built on a foundation of limestone rock from a nearby quarry. A plank floor was laid over the rock, easier on the feet of animals and easier to clean than a dirt or rock floor would have been. By the time the plank floor had worn out from use, concrete had come into use and gradually the floors were modernized. A windmill and tank a few feet to the north provided water for livestock. When electricity became available here in 1936, the water system was changed, but the windmill was left for use in emergencies.

The horses are long gone. The last team left with the advent of the first corn picker. Maud and Topsy, a beautiful, willing, matched team of roan Belgians, and Celia and Oscar, an ordinary team (one gray and one black, and smart enough to follow a corn row), were the last replaced by tractors.

The cattle are not stanchioned as they were when they came in 1909. Cattle sheds with feed and water handy replaced the use of barn space and feed boxes. Fencing now is different than it was 100 years ago. Modern feeding systems save time and energy. The wooden 30-

The Big Red Barn

foot silo, high as the barn roof, built in the early 1900s seemed a wonderful way to store winter feed but soon became obsolete and was taken down. Some hay still is stored in the mows for emergency feed, but most is fed ad lib from small bales on the ground, in the field, or from the big roll-around metal feeders.

Neighbors Gather for the Barnraising

Building the barn, or "raising" as it was called then, must have been very difficult. But then, as now, farm neighbors were helpful and prospects of a barnraising brought relatives, neighbors, friends, and the curious with all sorts of helpful suggestions. Much of the measuring, sawing, nailing (with square nails), the "flat work," had been done on the ground well in advance of the big day.

The lumber mills and yards in the Clinton-Fulton area just at the Narrows in the Mississippi River were getting into production by the mid-1850s. Big rafts of logs from the forests in Wisconsin, Minnesota and beyond, were lashed together and floated down the river where they were worked into required sizes and pieces at the lumber mills. So cheap was lumber that the beautiful, straight, long logs that outlined the rafts, and that had holes bored to thread the restraining cables through, were given away for the hauling rather than tow them back to the forests for the next load of logs downstream. The lumber needed for the big barn in 1856-57 was hauled here from the mills by wagon.

Skilled by experience, carpenters measured, cut, sawed, fitted and fastened many of the stress-bearing sections of the barn together with pegs, not metal connections. The ladder to the upper haymow is a work of art, not a nail in it, each rung tight and in place, just as it was made 129 years ago.

Perhaps one of the attractions for a barnraising was the good, homemade food brought for the big day by the women of the neighborhood, a rural custom that still prevails at any gathering in our community.

The big, wooden bins in the middle of the floor space in the barn that held the winter's supply of oats, wheat and barley are gone. In their place are two thousand-bushel corncribs that are filled each fall through a hole in the present galvanized steel roof that long ago replaced the wooden shingle roof.

The Big Red Barn

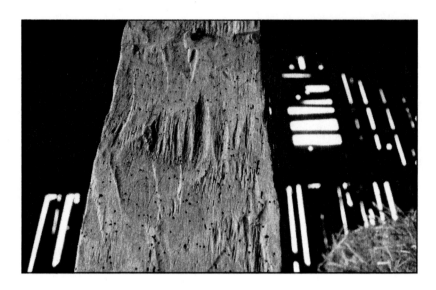

Handhewn timbers support the barn, sturdy since 1857; it still shelters livestock (and a few barn cats) on the Abbott farm.

Gunsmith Assists Underground Railroad

In addition to its usefulness as shelter for animals and feed, the old barn was a "station" on the Underground Railroad about the time of the Civil War. Asa Abbott, a son of the Benjamin Abbott who first bought this acreage, was born in Vermont, in 1820. As a young man, he worked at many jobs in the East and had learned the trade of gunsmith at the U.S. Arsenal in Springfield, Mass. He shipped a supply of gunsmithing tools west as far as the Mississippi River, by way of Kentucky, where he observed slavery as recorded in Harriett Beecher Stowes' book, "Uncle Tom's Cabin," so popular just before the Civil War. At Oquawka, Ill., Asa met Royce Oatman, who encouraged him to come North to ply his trade, saying there was no gunsmith between St. Louis and St. Paul and one was sorely needed in the vicinity of the "Narrows" at Fulton, Ill., where he had a cabin.

Asa and his wife, whom he had married at Oquawka and who was a sister of Oatman's wife, came to Fulton and set up his gun repair shop along the Fort Dearborn to Fort Leavenworth, Kansas, trail. It was a small, one-room shop with one window and one door; a small cabin in which they lived was a short distance away. Business was good in the shop. Local Indians and wagon trains with would-be settlers heading West or lured to California by the 1848 gold rush were his customers.

Asa was impressed with the good soil here and the absence of hilly, rocky, thin soil he had disliked in the New England states. He wrote to his father describing the conditions here, so Benjamin came the next year and made the $5.00 per acre purchase of 80 acres from the government in 1848.

Soon after the 1848 gold rush to California began, the Oatman family joined a wagon train and left to seek their fortune in the West, but Asa chose to continue gunsmithing and farming here. The tragic fate of the Oatman family is another story *(Editor's note: next in this collection.)*

Convinced of the evils of slavery he had read about and had observed first-hand in Kentucky, Asa determined to do all in his power to help any slave attempting to escape to reach Canada and freedom. Few written records were kept of a system devised to help runaway slaves that became known as the Underground Railroad. There were no rails, no trains, no cars, no timetables, no engineers or conductors. But there were enough sympathetic persons willing to risk a heavy fine and possible imprisonment to help in any way possible any slave to escape to Canada. Assisting or sheltering a runaway slave was a Federal offense, so no written records were kept, but with good luck many runaway slaves were moved slowly North to freedom, maybe only a few miles at a time, and usually under cover of darkness at night.

It is said that a slave who had run away from his master in the South, traveling on foot at night, often used streams to escape bloodhounds, which could not follow his scent in water. A white friend finding such a cold, wet, hungry, frightened person would give him food, shelter, and hide him until conditions were safe to pass him on North to the next known sympathizer. Such a negro would have made his way by wading, or by boat on the river to Fulton and would be brought here to the big barn and left, under cover of darkness. Here he would be given food and clothing, if needed, and hidden while he rested until conditions seemed right to pass him on to the next "Station." Some night, after a few days' rest, he might be hid in the bottom of a lumber wagon in some hay, the Abbott family would be loaded in as though going to a neighbor's to spend the evening with friends, and he would be taken to the next sympathetic family about six miles away. It was a slow, dangerous route to freedom, and not all of them made it.

While here waiting to be passed to the North, the slave always was alert to danger and remained hidden in the loose hay. At meal times, a hearty meal was placed in a pail or basket and hung on a peg in the big barn, out of reach of cats or dogs. The children were cautioned to return at once to the house so they could honestly say they had not seen a black person, if questioned. In an hour or so, they were sent back to get the empty container. No written record was kept of the number of black persons helped, but a "slave stick," a smooth, fifteen-inch stick of lumber, was notched for each one. The stick then was shoved down into the oats bin in the barn, just as any old stick might be, but all the family knew its importance. The stick, with its 28 notches now is in our basement, reminder of the great conflict that preserved the Union—and abolished slavery.

The 28 notches in this piece of oak represent each of the slaves sheltered in this barn, a station of the Underground Railroad.

2. Lilac Bush a Living Memorial to Oatman Family

May 1984

On a warm summer afternoon in 1850, Mrs. Royce Oatman walked along the path from her cabin home carrying a little lilac bush.

This year, 1984, the big lilac bush on Lincoln Road that was planted that day on the Fort Dearborn-Fort Leavenworth Trail is in blossom, lovely and fragrant as usual, a living memorial to the Royce Oatman family.

Oatman, a native of New York State, was a restless young man, and had been working his way West for some years. He married, and with his wife and family settled in Ustick Township in 1846. By 1850 the family consisted of father, mother and seven children, but the lure of gold in California was strong. They sold the cabin they had built and other belongings for about $1,500, and Mrs. Oatman loaded the covered wagon that was to be their home, and tried to pack into it things the family of nine would need for the next months until a new home could be established.

Now she was walking the half mile from the cabin, which is what is now the Abbott cow pasture, to the home of her sister, Mrs. Asa M. Abbott. She was bringing a farewell gift, a bit of the lilac bush she had set out at every home she had since leaving New York.

The sisters planted the little lilac bush that warm summer afternoon, and the next morning the Oatman family left to join a wagon train at Independence, Mo.

Seven families, about 50 persons, left Independence Aug. 9. Some turned back, one man died, differences arose, rations became scarce, the oxen and cattle tired; some were stolen by Indians as the little company went on.

Lilac Bush a Living Memorial to Oatman Family

By the time they reached New Mexico, having chosen the Southern route because they feared winter weather to the North, only the Oatmans and two other families remained. Oatman chose to continue but the other two families remained. He requested help in crossing the desert to Fort Yuma but the help was delayed and he pressed on alone.

At the Gila River, a band of Yavapai Indians attacked them, burned the wagon and killed all the family but three—Lorenzo, 15; Olive, 14; and Mary Ann, 8. Lorenzo was left for dead and the girls were taken captive to the Indian camp about 200 miles away.

Their suffering and captivity were unbelievable. Little Mary Ann died of starvation. Olive was sold a year later to the Mohave tribe and four years later was bought for two horses, a few blankets and beads, and released through the efforts of Lorenzo, who had survived the massacre and never had ceased in his search for his sisters.

Olive went first to benefactors in Oregon, then returned to Cottonwood (Hemlo) to the Abbott home, and for a few months attended the Cottonwood School. Later she attended an academy in the East. In 1865 she married Major John Fairchild in Rochester, N.Y. and they moved to Sherman, Texas, where she died in 1903.

The horrors of the massacre and captivity remained with her all her life. The tattoo marks on her face that branded her as a slave were very noticeable and always a source of ridicule or sympathy. The state of Arizona and the Historical Society have erected a suitable monument and fenced the site of the graves of the Oatmans, about six miles from Sentinel, 70 miles east of Yuma. In 1970, an official Texas grave marker for Olive was dedicated in Sherman.

Lorenzo worked in the Cottonwood area several years, later operating a hotel in Red Cloud, Neb., with help from his son, Roy. He died Oct. 8, 1901, age 65 years.

3. "Different" Callers

March 1981

In the old, Good Old Days when the first owner lived here, in the 1840s, transient callers were different, so they say. Indians, curious about what was done in the little gun repair shop along the Fort Dearborn-Fort Leavenworth Trail that now is U.S. 30 and more recently Lincoln Road, would walk into the shop, stand or sit without a word, observe, and leave. Often, an Indian, as he left, would pick up a piece of metal that he fancied and take it along only to find that it was heavier than he had supposed. It might be found by the owner where it had been dropped, sometimes only a few feet from the door, or further along the foot path that led off toward the creek a mile to the north, wherever it happened to get too heavy to be attractive. Even now, occasionally an odd piece of metal is found or plowed up in a pasture or cultivated field, evidence of the packrat trait of the noble red man.

Another story of the old, Good Old Days that happened a few miles north of here is that of the Indian brave who walked unannounced into the cabin of a settler and insisted to the terrified housewife that she trade her baby sleeping in the cradle for the papoose he was carrying. By words and actions, she finally persuaded him to leave. This happened several times, always when her husband was in the fields, and they concluded he had no intention of swapping babies, that he just enjoyed frightening the mother.

With the coming of the railroads to this part of the state in the 1850s, the tramps found an easier way than "counting steps" and "counted ties." Homes along the railroad and in the towns where the freights stopped were visited for lunches and handouts. In later years, as wagon roads developed into highways and drivers of cars might pick up a transient and give him a ride for a few miles, the tramps left the tracks and began stopping at farms along the roads for free meals.

"Different" Callers

The usual approach about meal time was a knock at the kitchen door and, "Have you got any work I could do for something to eat?" Nearly always the willingness to work could get a good meal. In those days every farm had a wood shed nearby, an ax and a chopping block to cut wood for the cook stove, and a tramp could get a meal for a few minutes work. If dinner was a bit late, or he worked extra hard there might be a bonus of a sandwich and some cookies in a sack to "take along." A few tramps might even chop a little more wood after dinner, without being asked to do so. But a few that stopped would leave without a word when asked to chop wood or rake, and the old men never were asked to work.

Our favorite "regular" was an old man headed west, who came along one afternoon as we were raking the front yard. He turned in the driveway and asked for a cup of coffee and a bite to eat. So we had lunch together while we rested and visited. Like many of the hobos, he wanted to talk about his travels. In the winter he spent the cold months in a sort of nursing home in New Jersey that his children thought was a good place for him. But he said that when Spring came he just couldn't stand all those old folks there any longer so he just packed up a few things in a sack and walked away. He was on his way to the west coast where he had some relatives in Washington.

That Fall, he stopped as we were working in the yard and said he was on his way back to the Home where he would live for the Winter and start out again when Spring came. Sure enough, he stopped the next Spring, but not that Fall. The third Spring, he knocked at the door and when we opened it looked at us accusingly and said, "I stopped last Fall for lunch and you weren't home."

4. Signs of Spring

March 1981

It won't be long now, a flock of north-bound geese, willow trees turning yellow, yard muddy, little pigs and wobbly legged calves, and Sunday noon a man tending a smoking charcoal grill near his back door.

In the Good Old Days, spring always brought bands of gypsies and tramps out of hibernation who took to the road. They differed, since gypsies traveled as families or as groups while tramps usually were loners. In the heyday of railroads and before automobiles, tramps followed the rails, boarding freights in the railroad yards, sleeping in box cars, mooching meals where and when hunger overtook them.

Gypsies, who traveled by horse-drawn vehicles, were confined to the roads and as nomads of the prairies lived off the land as they went along—trading horses, pilfering here and there, roasting ears and feed for their teams from corn fields along the way. Water being a necessity for their livestock, they usually camped along a stream near a town or close to farm buildings where they were viewed with suspicion. Children were cautioned to not go near them lest they be seized, hid in one of the wagons, and taken away never to be seen again by their loved ones.

Setting up camp near a village, women of a band often went to stores to beg. Clerks and proprietors hurried them out, but not before small items on the counters disappeared into the voluminous skirts and shawls the women wore. The women also wheedled their way into homes, offering to tell fortunes, and while the naïve housewife had her fortune told by a dusky soothsayer several others were quietly prowling the house and stealing what came handy.

Gypsies, like tramps, were tolerated by the public up to a point, and eventually hustled out of a community, on to the next

Signs of Spring

town—the next county—or over the bridge to Iowa, preferably without trouble with the law, which they seemed to respect when necessary.

The church at Cottonwood Corners had a long shed built nearby to shelter horses of the parishioners in inclement weather that was a favorite camp site for gypsy bands many, many years ago. The adjacent school yard had a well and hand pump; cornfields and gardens were close by for night time prowling. A horse with the heaves that had been picked up at a sale barn for almost nothing might be "doctored up" and palmed off on some unsuspecting farmer in the neighborhood, at a good price or swapped for a healthy one.

A few wagons camped one afternoon under the big elm tree to the east and about milking time a gypsy came begging for some fresh milk for one of their women who was sick and needed food. Later the man came back saying the woman was very sick and asking that we call a doctor. This was done, the doctor came out from Morrison and when the man came next morning for more milk he was jubilant—there was a brand new baby boy in the wagon at the corner.

About 70 years ago, a young man attending the University of Illinois *(Editor's note: L.A. Abbott)* contracted scarlet fever and after six weeks in the isolation hospital (pest house, in those days) was brought home to recuperate.

On Saturday, he stayed home to sleep and rest in bed while the family went to town to do the weekly shopping.

A band of gypsies camped near the big tree at the corner probably saw them leave, assumed everyone had gone away, and came to prowl. Finding the door unlocked, they came in and were ransacking the downstairs. The noise and their conversation wakened the convalescent who came down to see what was going on, and ordered them to leave. Observing that he was in no physical condition to enforce any orders, they laughed and continued to take things they wanted.

Luckily, a small fire extinguisher hanging on the wall was within reach. The young man grabbed it, opened the valve and turned it full force on the intruders. They dropped their sack of loot and fled.

Probably the best known tramp or hobo of the Good Old Days was "A-J" who is reported to have stopped here several times as he crisscrossed the country maintaining his reputation as the most famous professional tramp.

Signs of Spring

He was said to be rather courtly, polite, not too dirty a person, with a unique approach to mooching a meal.

Knocking at the kitchen door about dinner time, he would greet the lady of the house with a plea for a bit of hot water to make a cup of tea with the little sack of tea leaves he carried with him. This was nearly always granted and probably wherever he stopped, food was offered to go along with his tea.

Here, a place was set for him at the table and he enjoyed the same meal the family was eating. He confided that his little bag of tea leaves had got him many a good meal.

The original House by the Side of the Road at The Pines stood nearly a century, until replaced by a modern ranch house in the mid-1950s.

5. Where Hobos Sleep

March 1981

In the Good Old Days, when every little town had its own small jail, tramps often asked permission to sleep in the jail and it was usually granted. Others stopped at farm houses and asked to sleep in the barn at night. Usually this was allowed but a tramp was required to empty his pockets of matches and tobacco, which could be retrieved along with breakfast in the morning. Sleeping in a bed of nice clean hay wasn't too bad. Probably a good many tramps slipped into barns unnoticed for a night's rest.

In the days of the one-room schools, about the last thing the teacher did before leaving the building in late afternoon on cold days was to stoke the furnace with a few shovels of coal, cover it with ashes, and hope it would smolder along all night and keep the building warm. Her first job on arriving the next morning was to hurry down to the basement, shake down the ashes, add coal to the glowing coals and get things warm by the time the children arrived.

Imagine the astonishment of a Cottonwood School teacher (now living in Morrison), who unlocked the door, hurried down the basement stairs, and found a tramp cuddled up along the warm furnace. Tramps had reasoned that smoke from a school chimney meant a warm place to sleep, basement windows usually were not locked, entrance was easy, and they could be gone in the morning and no one would know they had been there. But this one overslept.

Many years ago, a crime had been committed one night in the Morrison area. The persons suspected were thought to have come in this direction and a farm-to-farm search was in progress. Sheriff Henry Hamilton asked permission to search the barns here and with the owner went carefully through all the buildings on the north side of the highway, but found nothing amiss. With their flashlights, they crossed the road to the cattle shed on the south side where a door that is always closed was open about a foot, indicating something out of order.

Letting themselves in cautiously, the men turned the powerful beam on two bicycles near the door and called for whoever was hiding to come out with hands up. Soon, two terrified boys, with hands over their heads, crawled out from among the bales of hay. About 14 years old, they soon established their identities. This being spring vacation, their parents had given them permission to take a bicycle trip to a town in eastern Iowa to visit relatives of one of the boys. They had made the trip there in one day and now were on their way home but had got caught in a shower and were delayed. Knowing they could not make it home to Dixon before dark, they saw this shed and decided to stay all night, get an early start and be home for breakfast. They were told to go back to bed among the hay bales, but next time to get permission and avoid trespassing.

6. "Workers" in Disguise

July 1981

During the Depression and Dust Bowl years, folks who thought they had their lives well organized and the future of their families assured found themselves without jobs and income, and forced to retrench in any way they could. Nothing like this had happened before. Farms that nearly were paid for produced too little to make the mortgage payment and banks foreclosed. Grasshoppers destroyed crops. Dust covered fields and fences. Pioneer villages became ghost towns. Anything marketable was sold for whatever it would bring— sometimes not enough to pay the shipping charges on livestock— hoping to hang on for another crop year and another chance.

Others simply gave up, packed their few belongings in the old car or truck, loaded up the family and headed back East where they had relatives who might help them find a job.

Late one fall afternoon, some 40 years ago, such an unfortunate man and his wife driving an old car loaded with household and camping equipment stopped here. They showed us pictures of their farm back in Kansas, dust drifted over the fences, the corn fields showing only a few barren stalks, dust as high as the window sills of their little cabin home, no sign of livestock anywhere. They said they were trying to get back to West Virginia where they had lived until the dream of a home "out west" lured them to Kansas.

They recommended themselves highly as farm help and would be glad to work at anything to earn enough to buy food and gas as they made their way east. If we could give them a job for a day or two they had their own camping and cooking equipment so would be no bother to us, they would be so grateful.

At that time, we had an orchard with fall apples ready to pick so we hired the man to work. They were offered a room in the house for sleeping and if the wife would help me with meals, they were

"Workers" in Disguise

welcome to eat with us. They accepted the offer of meals but preferred to use their own sleeping equipment. The big driveway of the corncrib was empty at the time so we suggested they use the corncrib as headquarters rather than pitch a tent outside, just in case of bad weather.

After breakfast the next morning, the picking ladder was put in the apple tree nearest the house, the man given a shoulder picking bag and he started to work. In about a half hour, he came limping to the house and said he had slipped off a rung of the ladder and hurt his back and would have to rest. This he did for three days, the limp disappeared but he still complained of pain.

In the meantime, trouble developed around the corncrib. They had brought with them from Kansas their dog, which felt very protective toward their belongings in the crib and guarded them closely. A feedyard full of cattle not used to dogs was next to the crib, and to get to their water tank the cattle had to pass the crib. The dog always barked furiously and spooked them.

It was suggested the dog be tied somewhere in the yard where it could not see the cattle. The woman was very fond of the dog, which would be "so lonesome," but when we were quite firm about moving the dog, the woman pouted and cried and refused to come to the house for meals. So, the man carried a tray of food out to her—and the dog. This went on for several days and we gradually got the idea that maybe they didn't want to work as much as was indicated they did when they came.

By the end of the week, we decided it was time they moved on. They were told that Monday morning their gas tank would be filled with gas, a lunch put up for their dinner and after breakfast they would be expected to leave. We watched them go, and before they had gone 40 rods, the car ran—or was driven—down into the ditch. Father got out the tractor, pulled them back onto the road, told them he would follow them as far as the edge of Morrison, and from there to West Virginia would be up to them.

7. Strawberry Fields

April 1981

The hard times of the Great Depression years of the '30s led to setting out a strawberry bed for extra income. This required more than family help at times when as many as 400 boxes could be picked a day.

Several folks who were walking by on the highway during the season and observed the activity stopped to ask for a job for a day or two and were hired for meals, lodging and a few cents a box for what they picked. Most of them "got a backache" after a day of stooping and crawling along in the hot sun and quit, but several lasted longer.

A nice, young man who claimed to be a student attending Harvard University told us he was from England and was spending the vacation walking to the west as far as he could go and make the return trip before classes resumed in the fall. He planned to work enough to pay his way, if possible, and so far had been able to do so, was seeing the United States agriculture first hand and enjoying it.

Another who asked for a job was a young woman driving an old car. She told us she was on her way west, perhaps as far as California, where she hoped to get bookings for a dog act she had developed with about a half dozen dogs accompanying her. She was hired and stayed a few days.

Evenings, tired as we all were, we enjoyed sitting in the yard for the "Show" as she put the dogs through their tricks to keep them in practice. The dogs were various breeds, most of the eight were small dogs, in good condition and well trained. They walked a tight rope, played ball, could count, tumble, do the dog tricks one usually sees in a circus and seemed to enjoy it.

A man asking for work that summer offered to do anything for a job, seemed to really want to work and was hired for field work. He was good help, clean around the house, willing to do anything, and offered to paint if needed, so he stayed on after corn plowing. He told us almost nothing about himself but from little things he said we guessed he might have some farm background, had been living in Chicago were he had joined a painter's Union, got out of favor with the Union and was hiding out until the trouble blew over.

In the hot summer evenings, we usually sat out on the porch to cool off, read the papers and rest. His interest was in the Chicago Tribune, especially any news of labor Union unrest, and if a car drove into the yard he disappeared immediately as if afraid to be seen. John stayed with us until fall when suddenly he announced that he guessed it was safe to go back and he'd like to ride along the next day with the cattle truck that was to leave for Chicago. He went in the next evening and asked to be let off near the Stockyards, where he seemed familiar with the surroundings.

One wonders about folks one knows for a few days or a few weeks. What became of them? Where are they now? Did they find their dreams?

8. Anonymous Callers

September 1981

We wonder sometimes about some of the folks who have stopped at the House by the Side of the Road. Have we, maybe, been entertaining angels unawares? Or perhaps a spy? An undercover FBI person? A future Fannie May?

The Great Depression brought an unusual caller about the middle of a gloomy, late fall day. She was a middle-aged woman, clean, plainly dressed and energetic. She had tied her quiet, white horse, hitched to an old top buggy, to the fence at the road. In the good old days, every house yard had a fence at the road because cattle, and sometimes hogs were driven on foot to the stockyards at Union Grove for shipment by rail, on the Chicago and Northwestern, to the Chicago market.

When we answered her knock at the door she asked if she could use the cookstove to make some candy. She had pans and spoons and all the necessary ingredients, just needed a stove to cook on. She said she was on her way to the southwestern states for the weather and was financing the journey be selling homemade candy along the way. Nobody had much money at the time, but some folks could find a few cents for a bit of candy.

So we brought in another basket of cobs for the cookstove, she carried in her equipment from the buggy, and went to work making fudge. With two batches going at once she soon had enough to package about a dozen small sacks. Washing the sticky pans was done quickly. She declined an offer to unhitch and put the horse in the barn, have supper, and stay all night, saying she was anxious to get to the Mississippi River at East Clinton by dark, apparently knowing exactly the route she intended to follow. She had a pail to water the horse, a pan for its grain, and tethered it along the road to graze during the night. For herself, she had food, a small pup tent and blankets, and in bad weather could sleep in the buggy, which had a rolldown oilcloth cover for the front.

We supposed she would be in Iowa early the next morning, peddling the candy, and finding another cookstove somewhere along the way for the next batch. We were surprised to learn she had stayed in East Clinton for more than a week with a sympathetic family, had made and sold a little of the candy and seemed in no hurry to move on. She made several trips across the bridge to Clinton to sell candy and exhibited much interest in the wagon bridge and the railroad bridge, train schedules and traffic, and the draw bridge.

So soon after World War I, her lengthy stay and interest in the bridges and the traffic they carried was viewed with suspicion. Was she an undesirable person perhaps mapping a strategic point for bombing in case of war? Or was she what she seemed to be, just a harmless future Fannie May trying to make a living?

During the war, a man and a woman pushing a baby buggy with a baby in it, blankets and considerable luggage in the buggy had been apprehended on the highway as spies. Inspection of the baby buggy showed the "baby" to be a very life-like doll. The blankets and luggage concealed cameras, and exposed film of vulnerable places along the route were confiscated. Such an outfit was seen traveling east past here but did not stop.

A few weeks after the assassination of Martin Luther King Jr., in Memphis, a very black man stopped one hot afternoon and asked for a drink of water from the well at the back door. It was such a hot, sunny day; Father, who was working nearby, joined him as he sat on the well platform in the shade of the apricot tree and enjoyed the cool drink. The visitor was very well dressed, apparently well educated, was riding an expensive English bicycle, and in no hurry to be on his way. He talked for more than an hour, describing the killing in detail, insisting the man who pulled the trigger was black, and wondered what we might have heard or thought about the assassination.

We learned that he stayed in the Morrison and Round Grove community for about a week, ate his meals in the local restaurants, seemed to have plenty of money, talked with folks, rode his bike on many streets and roads, had no particular reason for remaining in the area, and finally moved on. Was he just a pleasant, black man on a bicycle tour, on his vacation, enjoying the friendliness of a small

Anonymous Callers

Midwestern community, or was he an FBI man on a hot trail, or perhaps an NAACP member getting the feeling of northern rural folks on the unfortunate happening in the South?

One of the first stories we recall about this road was told by Mrs. Della Bull Goff many years ago.

As a little girl, she lived with her parents on the farm now owned and operated by the Siefken family about a half mile west of Cottonwood Corners. Just east of the buildings, a small stream crossed the road and pioneers going West in their covered wagons often camped there overnight so the horses could drink, graze and rest in the late afternoon shade in the summer.

In the evening, the farm family often visited with the wagon family around their campfire, exchanging news and stories and experiences, making friends. She remembered how the children used to sit on the double-tree of the wagons, listening spellbound to the tall tales of Indians, and gold, and adventure. Singing around the campfire was part of an evening's pleasure. She first heard the new song, "Oh Suzanna" on such an evening, and learned the tune and the words from the travelers.

9. Traveling Sales

April 1981

In the days before automobiles, when deliveries were made with horses and wagons instead of trucks, peddlers of various goods ran regular routes through the rural area, stopping at farm houses to sell their wares for cash or to bargain with the housewife for butter, eggs or other products.

Among the first of the grocery wagons with its stock of staple needs such as sugar, flour, yeast, coffee, tea, salt, corn meal and oatmeal was one from Balk's Store in Fulton. Balk's wagon, like all the other grocery wagons, gradually increased its stock and the business thrived through honesty and hard work of the family. The little store became a big store that in time passed from father to son and flourished for many years until replaced by supermarkets.

Another regular visitor who came about twice a year was the Watkins Man, purveyor of patent medicines in bottles, boxes and cans. Probably there were other brands, but Watkins was the name heard most often. Favorites in many households were vanilla, lemon, and maple flavorings for baking and cooking, liniment for man or beast, and cough syrup.

All of those products were put up in bottles holding about a pint. On the side of the bottle was "Sample Line." The purchaser was urged to try the product down as far as the sample line and if not satisfied it could be returned and the cost refunded at the next visit.

One wonders what became of the bottles which were returned with about one fourth used. Were they just filled and put in circulation again? Where was the Pure Food and Drug Act then? Or were some of them used below the sample line, filled to the line and returned for the refund?

Salves and ointment to cure many bruised and sore spots, lotions and powders also were offered by Watkins. In later years, as

Traveling Sales

Watkins traveled by car, other products were added. The handiest little jar and lid opener ever invented was an item an enterprising Watkins Man sold as a sideline for a quarter.

The scissor grinder and the umbrella mender stopped at long intervals. The Rags, Old Iron and News Paper Man came once, sometimes twice a year, spring and fall to buy those items. Children of farm families often had collected a pile of junk iron discards from machinery, nails, a sack or two of old rags and worn out clothes, empty bottles, or bundles of paper. These were weighed on a small scale and paid for by the pound. The children received the money for the trash they had collected, never more than a dollar or two. But that was a lot of money in the good old days that could mean a ride on the merry-go-round at the Fair or a new pencil and tablet for school.

In the Great Depression years, when men who had good jobs suddenly found themselves out of work, there was not unemployment compensation of any kind to cushion the jolt. Those with ambition to find some way to earn a living tried many ideas.

One who had worked for years at a factory started a route, on foot, selling homemade rolls his wife baked, walking some 20 miles every day to take home a dollar. There was little market for such bargains since farm produce had fallen to near zero, banks were closed and no one had any money. Eggs were three cents a dozen, dressed frying chickens were three for a dollar or four live chickens for a dollar, strawberries three quarts for a quarter.

Folks who lived along the river came to the door selling fish for 10 cents a pound, beautiful big catfish. Others came hoping to sell articles they had made from the willow trees that grew so abundantly along the river—children's little arm chairs, little tables, plant stands, whistles, knick knacks of all sorts made from the willow twigs. They were strong and well made with no investment but a few nails and a lot of time.

Some folks came trying to sell things made from scrap wire—cake racks, tool racks, folding wire baskets, fancy designs. Had we had money to buy them, we now might have some antiques, relics of really hard times.

10. Rainy Days and Pianos

April 1981

The Watkins Company shared with other retailers the idea that if a prospective customer could just be persuaded to try the product there was a good chance a sale could be made. In the Good Old Days when a fine big upright piano was a status symbol in the home, furniture dealers, who often carried musical instruments also in their stock, figured a way to use the try-buy schemes, and sometimes it worked.

Merchants in small towns had a good idea as to which farm families could afford pianos, especially those with small children or young ladies with a bit of musical ability as demonstrated in church work. And so it was that a dealer who made deliveries with a team and wagon used the try-buy scheme to get the farm family and the piano together.

It worked best during the spring and summer months when thunderstorms came up suddenly, yet left time enough to drive from Fulton or Morrison to a farm a few miles away. Loading a piano onto the wagon, the dealer and his helper would set forth when a thunderstorm seemed to be heading their way and drive slowly toward the farm they had chosen. Keeping an eye on the storm's approach, they could time their arrival just ahead of the rain. Dashing on the run into the farm yard, the dealer ran to the door and begged of the astonished housewife permission to unload this very fine and valuable piano into the house, or if that were not possible, could they PLEASE get it into a barn or some other shelter since it simply must not get wet! Any place in the house would do, just some out of the way corner, they would be so grateful for any kind of shelter.

Farm folks, then as now, anxious to help someone in need, usually urged them to hurry and bring it into the house, "just set it right over here in this corner of the parlor," (where she probably often had thought a piano might look nice). By this time rain might be coming down in torrents, the men of the family had come into the house to rest during the shower and have a lunch, which of course the dealer and his helper were invited to share. This gave him the chance he needed to expound on the qualities and desirability of this fine instrument, and being a play-by-heart musician himself, he would demonstrate the tone and ease of making music with "Turkey in the Straw," or if the family was known to be very religious, he played well-known hymns or patriotic songs. The children and other family members were urged to try the piano to prove its worth.

As the storm moved on, the dealer suggested that since it now was so damp outside and his wagon so wet, it would be much appreciated if he could leave it here for a few days and pick it up again in a week or so when the weather was better. He wanted them to use it and enjoy, invite their friends in for a "sing" if they liked, just anything to show his appreciation of their kindness. And so the piano and the customer had a week to get acquainted.

Usually by the end of the week, the family had been sold on the idea of buying the piano, especially when the dealer offered a "discount" from the price he had taken pains to mention, in an offhand manner, on his first visit. This clinched the deal, and another farm family had a status symbol in the parlor.

11. Stalled at Sundown

July 1981

Living in a house by the side of a transcontinental highway, perhaps we get more pleas for help than folks who live on a side road or down a lane. Those who are stalled toward sundown for one reason or another seem to be in more distress than those who are stranded earlier in the day.

Help is likely to be more available at chore time when the men of the family are in from the fields and are more knowledgeable about flat tires, cracked radiators, leaky hoses, dirty spark plugs and such things than the women of the family are, and get the unlucky travelers on their way before dark.

During the Depression days there were many vehicles on the road that were hardly fit to be there. One such pulled up to the driveway about chore time one chilly fall day and a woman came to the front door and told us the car just refused to run, and was there a man around that could help her husband get it going again?

We called Father from the barn to help, and the woman asked if the children in the car could come in to get warm while the men were busy with the car. We said they might, she went to the door, let out a whoop that could have been heard a mile—"Come on in, kids, she says we can." Doors on the car burst open and five children from toddlers to teenagers raced to the house, and in five minutes had made themselves completely at home.

The men gave up on the repair job and called a dealer in Clinton who handled that make of car and said he might be able to fix it, but would not try unless it was brought to him, since it was already past closing time.

Meantime, in the house, things were going from noisy to noisier, everyone was hungry. So we hurriedly peeled more potatoes, cut more slices of ham, opened another two-quart jar of the pears we had been canning that day, cut two loaves of bread and set the table for seven extra. Father finished chores and faced with the problem of sleeping arrangements for the night for seven extras, he offered to tow the car and family to Clinton to the garage where the mechanic would work on the car.

So after supper they left for Clinton where the mechanic located the trouble but could not fix it that night. The family's plight was reported to the police department and help from the Red Cross and Salvation Army—two organizations that often were called on to help stranded motorists—was enlisted to provide beds and breakfast the next morning.

Such encounters were not always so pleasant. A neighbor who lived in a house by the side of the road told us of two couples who came to the door one cold night. Their car had broken down, and they asked if they could stay all night. They were allowed sleeping rooms upstairs.

In the morning, one of the women, who apparently had gone through at least one bureau or dresser drawer during the night came downstairs with a package of human hair she had found in the drawer. In the good old days, women wore their hair long, and those who had luxuriant hair might cut it to have a switch made just in case illness or some other misfortune might thin her hair. Or, very fine hair, particularly grey or white hair, could be sold at a high price.

The woman told the lady of the house she was a maker of such switches and would be glad to make it up for her at no cost to repay the family for the night's lodging. She was allowed to take the hair when they left. That was the last the owner ever saw of the hair—or their "guest."

12. Car Troubles Along the Road

February 1981

Out of Control

Probably in the last few decades since automobile travel has become common, every fence along every field bordering a transcontinental highway has been damaged by some vehicle out of control.

In the Good Old Days, yard fences were necessary to keep livestock from wandering into unprotected places. Usually folks on horseback or on foot preceded the cattle, sheep or hogs and blocked lanes and unfenced areas, and farm driveways. Most yards now are not fenced along the road for easier lawn mowing.

Hearing a crash one autumn day many years ago, we ran to the door in time to see a Model T dragging out a stout corner post, its two brace posts and several rods of woven wire at the entrance to our driveway. The driver, a middle-age man, came in to the house to telephone relatives for help.

While he waited for them to come, we dressed a few superficial wounds, patched him up with band-aids and served some hot coffee. As he relaxed, he enumerated the repairs he would have to make on his car, his own discomfort and inconvenience, and the cost of his accident. As he was about to leave, we said: "Well, how about fixing our fence?" and he looked at us in disgust and said, "Lady, after all the trouble I've had today you don't expect me to fix your fence, too, do you?"

Soon after it was repaired, we heard a car—Model Ts made more noise then than cars do now—and saw a car circling and circling the apple tree in the front yard. Then it was out of the driveway and down the highway. Recognizing the driver as a neighbor, we called her to see if she had had an accident. She explained that she hadn't driven for quite a while and had intended to stop but couldn't remember just how to do it so went home. We wondered how she stopped when she got home.

Perhaps like one of our neighbors who, as most farmers then did, kept his car in the driveway of the corncrib. Trying out a newer model, he couldn't stop it in the crib so drove on out the opposite door and around again but still hadn't caught on in time to stop in the crib at the usual spot. After a few more unsuccessful trips through the crib, he called to his wife to come and shut the door at the far end as soon as he drove in the front door and trap the new car.

Mailboxes go for a Spin

Mr. Murray's choice of the Sam Walter Foss poem, "The House by The Side of the Road" for his Cabbages and Kings column last week is thought-provoking to one who has lived in such a place for a long time. Practically, life there can be less than ideal. For instance, when we glanced out the kitchen window Saturday morning something seemed different—a vacancy where usually there are mailboxes at the end of the driveway.

Sure enough, post, plank, and two big metal mailboxes were not there. Two men were in the yard looking over the situation. The post was broken off a few inches above the ground, the plank was a few feet east, the one box a rod further on, the other box a few rods toward the middle of the yard and the post far down the road, in the ditch.

Having had mailboxes broken off before, when one was replaced several years ago, the butt end of a telephone or utilities pole was used and set about four feet in the ground—a really solid installation. A piece of heavy plank several feet long held the boxes, all designed to discourage the average Hallowe'en mailbox tipper. The vehicle used must have got quite a jolt as pieces of metal were found along the tire tracks in the snow, in the ditch, and back onto the road.

Running Out of Gas

Nearly every person who drives a car has some time or other run out of gas. In the Good Old Days when gas was about 15% of its present price, most farmers had a gas barrel and could supply a gallon or two to help a stranded motorist get to the next gas station. But no more! With the switch to diesel fuel for tractors, the best the person who knocks at the door in the middle of the night can hope for is an offer to "use the telephone and call your friend to bring you some gas."

One nice Monday washday while hanging clothes on the line in the front yard, a car stopped a few rods to the east of the driveway and we saw a young man get out and walk back. He said he seemed to be out of gas and would like to buy some if we could help him out, so we quit hanging up clothes, got the new gas can just purchased and put in two gallons. He said his buddy in the car had their money to pay for it and he'd bring it when he returned the can. So we watched him put the gas in the car, throw the can in the car, jump in and take off, going east at top speed.

Maybe if it hadn't been a busy Monday morning, or he hadn't lied about the money for the gas, or hadn't stolen that brand new gas can it wouldn't have seemed so bad. A quick telephone call to the Sheriff's office in Morrison caught the car as it was going through town and netted quite a haul. The car had been stolen in Indiana, the set of burglary tools and stolen articles in the car proved that the men were wanted there and were held for the authorities and we got back our gas can.

Then there was the nice, young man who drove a delivery truck for a Clinton firm, who stopped one evening about chore time and was so sorry, he was out of gas, could we let him have enough to get to town? He had no authority from the company ever to pay for anything but would stop the next night on his route home and leave a voucher for the amount, if that would be satisfactory. And, as long as it was getting late to stop at a station for more, could we just as well let him take a five-gallon can full instead of a one gallon? Yes, we did. That was about 30 years ago, and he hasn't stopped yet! By the grapevine we found out that he had worked that same scheme on nearly every farm on his route. But there was one thing in his favor— he always returned the can.

No wonder farmers have switched to diesel fuel.

13. Roadside Trash

July 1981

Human nature hasn't changed much when it comes to discarding garbage. Observing an empty, brown glass beer bottle someone had thrown on our lawn close to the west driveway reminded us of an incident that happened at the same spot nearly 60 years ago, about noon on a misty late summer Sunday.

A carload of folks pulled into the driveway and appeared to be eating a picnic dinner in the car because of the damp weather. Soon the shells from hardboiled eggs were tossed out, then came wrappers from sandwiches and other things. As the meal progressed, paper plates and cups were discarded. Before the rinds from the watermelon we had seen them cutting could be ready to throw away, our father-in-law *(Editor's note: Alfred N. Abbott)*, a quiet, tactful man strolled down to the car.

He greeted the visitors politely, remarking on the poor picnic weather. They agreed, and explained that they had intended to find a nice park somewhere but so far had seen none. Since the kids all were hungry, and it was about noon, they decided to stop some place that had nice trees and grass and have their dinner, even though it did mean eating in the cramped quarters in the car.

He inquired where they were from—had they driven quite a ways? Yes, they lived in Rockford—do you know where that is? Yes—in what part of Rockford do you live? They named a street and, when asked, the house number, which he noted on a scrap of paper from his overall pocket. He assured them he knew exactly where that was as he had worked for some time on the Exemption Board only a few blocks away and was well-acquainted with that part of the city.

After further pleasant conversation, all the while melon rinds were being tossed on the ground, he told them that meeting them had been interesting and that some Sunday he and his wife might pack a

Roadside Trash

Roadside Trash

picnic lunch and drive to Rockford, park in their driveway, and leave their garbage on the lawn at their house, smiled and walked away.

They got the message, gathered up every scrap of garbage and took it with them when they left.

Now, if we just knew where to leave the brown beer bottle?

Ed Abbott's 1955 Ford alongside the Lincoln Highway--$2000, new.

14. Smokehouse Samaritans

Circa April 1981

In the Good Old Days, before electricity, lockers and home freezers kept a farm family supplied with summer meat, many farmers did their own butchering and preserved the meat for future use by canning and smoking. Pork chops could be fried and layers of the meat, covered with freshly rendered lard, kept for a few weeks in a cool place. Casings were stuffed with sausage of various kinds made from trimmings. The hams, pork shoulders and sausages were hung in a small building called the smokehouse and carefully smoked with a smoldering fire to just the right flavor, which took several weeks.

The smokehouse here was a small building about eight by ten feet, with walls of limestone rocks, dirt floor, wooden roof, a door and a tiny window. The roof was of wood and shingles, about six feet above ground, with rafters inside spaced to accommodate meat suspended with twine above the smoke from the little bonfire on the floor. A supply of dry wood to replenish the fire was kept there, also.

One day about this time of year, the family was eating dinner at noon when a loud knock at the back door was heard and a man opened the door and shouted, "There's a building in your yard on fire." Everyone jumped from the table, the men ran out, we grabbed a dish towel and tied the baby in the high chair securely in place, and ran out, too. Sure enough, smoke was pouring from every crack in the smokehouse, much more than a stick or two usually added could have produced. Everyone, including the man who had alerted us, and the woman in the car, carried water from the cattle tank to douse the fire that had spread to the dry wood. The flames had not reached the roof or the twine and meats, so not much damage had been done.

In all the excitement, no one noticed when the couple in the car left. We had no idea who they were and always regretted we did not get to thank them for saving our summer's supply of meat that year.

Wheat Field on Hon. A. N. Abbott's Farm, Ustick Twp., Whiteside Co., Ill.

A.N. Abbott surveys the wheat field on the former Oatman land near the south border of the farm, in a 1904 postcard. He's looking east-northeast, toward the homestead; later, this became a cow pasture.

15. What's in Your Garage?

October 1981

In the Good Old Days when the Model T replaced the horse and buggy, some place had to be found to keep the vehicle, and on the farm it was the driveway of the corncrib. It wasn't considered safe to have anything with so much gas in it close to the house.

After a few months of cranking the car by hand, of course, every time the crib was needed for its original purposes, usually a small shed was built or a lean-to added on another building to house the car. Now, several generations later, cars five times as big, with gas tanks in proportion, and costing ten times a much, have cozy homes in attached garages with a light that comes on when the automatic door opener is activated.

But there is a drawback to this. Being a part of the house, some good housekeepers insist on having the walls and ceiling covered in plywood, or painted, so the garage as seen from the outside is presentable, clean and orderly. After a few months of losing this battle, the average good housewife gives up, and the garage gradually becomes the repository of many things that are "too good to throw away" or "we might need this some time," and the car is in danger of being crowded out by just plain junk.

Then the decree goes out some rainy morning, "This is a good day to clean the garage." It isn't just discards from the house, but also the things brought in from outside that make up the clutter—the sack of walnuts to be shucked, late vegetables from the garden to be saved from frost, tools of all kinds—big and little, here and there—rakes, hoes, shovels, boards of all kind, five old tires, paint cans almost empty, part of a roll of roofing; that's what this story will be about.

Added to the list of things "too good to throw away" is a row of flower pots of many sizes, stacked three or four deep on the concrete foundation that holds the studding. On top of the cupboard and

What's in Your Garage?

destined for discard this time, is a basket of only slightly chipped and cracked flower pots and saucers. What to do with the pile in the corner of 14 grocery bags of newspapers, each sack neatly tied with twine to make it easier for the paper drive that never came this fall?

Cleaning a garage on a rainy day may not be such a good idea. It uncovers the things that were saved "to do something with" that there never seems time enough to do: the lawn chair that needs new webbing and a new screw; the two round-back wooden chairs that were going to be refinished for sure last summer; a bushel basket (and that's a real antique now, that used to be the container along with a bushel of anything, to be used when emptied, by the housewife as a clothes basket) that's now full of dried small flowers and leaves for making winter bouquets. And the bunches of Dusty Miller, moon money or silver dollar, pampas grass, milkweed pods, pussy willows, sea oats and pin oak leaves hanging on any nail that was handy. And the catnip drying for the cats. Why do we save SO MUCH?

Then there are treasures on another wall—the fishing dip net we got at a rummage sale but never used; the old copper wash boiler, black on the bottom from years of use over a cob fire in the cookstove.

Maybe we've cleaned enough for one day. It's time for lunch anyway, and while we have a glass of milk and a few cookies we can think about the Good Old Days when that wash boiler was filled with soft water from the cistern every Sunday night and the homemade bar of soap cut in to soften until morning. The stove was filled with cobs and a crumpled newspaper, enough to light early Monday morning. One had to get an early start or the washing wouldn't be drying on the line and dinner ready by noon, and the clean sheets back on the beds and the ironing done before time to do chores and get supper. Makes one appreciate electricity, automatic washers and dryers, detergents and perma-press bedding and clothing.

Another rainy day, we really should get that wall cleaned today. Beside the old copper wash boiler is a wash board, one of the real old-fashioned kind, with a place at the top for a bar of soap, and a corrugated rubbing surface of metal, zinc, perhaps. It was big enough to lay a dirty coverall leg on to be scrubbed with a stiff brush. The very first boards were all wood, corrugated, but wood became splintered after a few years' use, and metal replaced it. The deluxe model that came out much later had corrugated glass on the scrubbing area.

What's in Your Garage?

A few years ago, when dried bouquets became popular and homes began to have recreation and family rooms, folks wanted "conversation pieces," and old wash boards that probably cost less than a dollar would bring at a sale as much as a used davenport and chair set. The happy purchaser could then spend hours creating just the right arrangement for any season of the year he/she fancied, and installing it on the wash board to display to envious friends as a wall plaque.

Next to the wash board's spot on the wall hangs one of the two galvanized wash tubs handy for lots of things: cooling dressed chickens, cooling boiled corn for the freezer, holding a mess of live fish until they can be cleaned. *(Editor's note: A swimming pool for youngsters, too.)* We recall one huge catfish that had been caught in a private pond, on a fishing invitation, that was too big for the tub and hung over both sides—it was over three feet long. A small son of the host reported to his father that, "That man caught the biggest bullhead I ever saw."

The other tub—there were always two, one for rinsing and the other for bluing—now is on one end of the worktable, just right for the supply of cracklings, bought periodically for cat food, from the Fulton Locker.

Among the other things on the work table are three glass kerosene lamps, minus chimneys. With the coming of electricity to this part of the county about 45 years ago, housewives were glad to empty the bowls of the long-handled lamps, and quit forever the daily chore of washing the lamp and lantern chimneys along with the breakfast dishes every morning.

Snow on the ground discouraged further cleaning of the garage, so that project is continued until some rainy day next April. But we did get rid of a few things "too good to throw away" and re-located some others. By Spring more may accumulate. If everyone really discarded things there wouldn't be antiques.

Live Visitors in the Garage

You may think you know what's in your garage, but don't be too sure, even though you insist the door be kept shut as soon as the car is in or out. There's an old saying that a hole as big as one's little finger will admit a mouse, and our trap line yielded three in November.

What's in Your Garage?

Our neighbor says while her husband opened the door to tell her it was raining, a mouse ran in.

It took us ten minutes on a hot summer day last summer to dislodge a little garter snake that sneaked in and hid under the freezer when the Boss came in from outdoors.

Just inside the garage we keep a bushel basket in which we deposit tin cans, grass, stalks, paper, junk of all sorts that we find when we go to the mailbox. When the basket is full, the contents are emptied into the incinerator and burned.

Noting that the basket was about full, we picked it up and started for the burner, but dropped it hurriedly when something stirred in the basket. A snake, maybe? Poking into the contents uncovered a very live opossum playing 'possum, which somehow had found its way in when the big door must have been open too long, found this nice big basket of dried debris and settled in for a nap.

And then there was another neighbor who went to her garage to get the car and found a very live six-foot bull snake neatly draped, half on one side and half on the other, hanging down from a rafter just over the car. Makes one wonder just what is in the garage.

Illiniwek, pride of the Abbott herd, brought home the Herald trophy as grand champion steer at the 1950 Quad County Show, for showman Ed Abbott.

16. L.A. Abbott & Sons, Registered Herefords

Circa 1967

When the fourth generation of Abbotts interested in Hereford cattle look over the herd in 1967 for a good 4-H beef project they are likely to hear Dad or Grandpa explain the theory that "if it doesn't pay to keep good cattle, it sure doesn't pay to keep poor ones." That has been the policy since A.N. Abbott, in an effort to upgrade rather nondescript cattle on the farm west of Morrison, bought a purebred Hereford bull calf in 1906. It was bred by a neighboring firm, Parnham and Norrish, on the farm now operated by the Keith Jones family.

Convinced of the value of purebred livestock, two bred heifers were bought in 1909 from John Secor of Mechanicsville, Iowa, and in 1911 three cows with calves at foot and rebred were bought from Warren T. McKray of Kentland, Ind. From this beginning and keeping most heifer calves to add to the herd, the number increased and quality improved with good bulls bought from established herds.

One of the first practical lessons learned in the early 1900s was that all bull calves could not be sold as future herd bulls, but did make steers much superior to those raised from grade cows and grade bulls of various colors and breeding.

In the early years, a good bull was replaced by his son; a new bull of a different family line being brought into the herd every six or seven years to offset the tendency to inbreed. It took about 20 years to grow and retain a herd of 25 to 30 brood cows that up to 1929 would wean a 98% calf crop.

L.A. Abbott & Sons, Registered Herefords

Lean Years

Then disaster struck via brucellosis and all cows but two aborted and nearly 60% became barren, proving as a Disney cartoon contends, "It ain't all profit in the butcher business."

The herd was tested in 1931 and all but two reacted. Tests were made every six months and reactors sent to market. The herd was in quarantine from 1930 to 1941 when another epidemic of brucellosis hit and 50% were sent to market. That year, veterinarians began to vaccinate with Strain 19 and there has been no trouble since from contagious abortion. The herd never has had a T.B. reactor and no brucellosis reactor for 26 years.

Occasionally, a promising heifer or cow was added to the early herd to keep, re-sell or show. Animals were exhibited at local fairs from 1912 to 1917 until the World War I emergency tied up the supply of freight cars for transportation of cattle. Trucks for transportation of livestock did not come into general use for several years and during the middle '20s cattle were shown only at Morrison. There they could be driven on foot or freighted on a short haul from Union Grove.

Some cattle were sold in Association sales from 1919 through 1927. The state-wide, half-ton calf contest was developed in the 1920s, and in 1927 an Abbott calf, Kayo, was entered. He tipped the scales at 1,015 pounds the day he was one year old and sold later with some other steers 4 to 6 months older for $18.50 per cwt., the highest peacetime price paid for cattle on the Chicago market up to that time.

New Partners

Over the years the firm name changed from A.N. Abbott to A.N. Abbott & Son in 1914, when L.A. Abbott was graduated from the University of Illinois College of Agriculture, and returned to the home farm and partnership with his father. That firm name continued until 1944 when William and Edward Abbott were taken into partnership and the firm became L.A. Abbott & Sons, as it is now.

When Bill and Ed started in 4-H club work, each was given annually a steer calf and feed. Gross income from the sale of the steers was invested in securities toward a college fund. When the heifer program was added, each was given a heifer per year, which was retained in the herd and the accumulation credited to the boys. Sale of calves from these cows plus proceeds of the steer calf investments paid

L.A. Abbott & Sons, Registered Herefords

their entire expenses while students at the University of Illinois, supplemented by jobs at the beef and dairy barns, waiting on tables, washing dishes, setting pins at the bowling alley, etc. Bill graduated in agriculture in 1949 and Ed in 1952, third generation Illini, their grandfather, A.N., having been a member of the class of 1885. Ed was a member of the University's livestock judging team his junior year and since has judged many fairs and local shows.

Both Bill and Ed enjoyed 4-H work, Bill going to Club Congress on a conservation project and both holding local club and county offices during their years of membership. Both appreciated the chance to compete at the Quad County livestock show in Clinton, Iowa. As 10-year-olds, the water fights in the alley behind the old Coliseum where the first shows were held seemed more important than washing the calf. Along about the junior year in high school, when their math teacher released them for "cow convention" competition, grooming for the big show took on real importance.

Recognizing the link between good beef herds in the area and good feeders in the Quad-County feedlots, heifers were added in 1944 to the Quad County Show, which by that time had earned more than local attention and was known as the Little International. With heifers from the herd, Bill exhibited the champion Hereford heifer in 1945, and Ed the champions in 1947 and 1948. In his last year of club work, Ed received the Clinton Herald trophy for grand champion steer with Illiniwek, also an animal from the family herd.

Bill received a portion of the herd when he began farming and still maintains registration on animals although his emphasis now is dairying on his farm north of Fulton. He is active in farm organizations and leader of the Fulton 4-H'ers club. The herd on the home farm was maintained at 30 to 35 cows from 1941 to 1955 when Ed returned from overseas service and since has been increased to about 50 cows of breeding age.

Better Breeding, Better Performance
Recent herd sires have been Anxiety Donation 10, bought from Earl Haring, DeWitt, Iowa, Onward Abounds 44 from Slim Meyer, Bellevue, Iowa, WHG Regent 1 and WHG Regent 3 from Walter Greip, DeWitt, Iowa, CF Regent Heir from Clifford Feldman, West Liberty, Iowa, L13 Piegan 64 from Lee Bros., Letts, Iowa, and SC

L.A. Abbott & Sons, Registered Herefords

Silver Anxiety 1 from Milton Edleman, Webb, Iowa. The latter bull is owned in partnership with Bickelhaupt Herefords, Mt. Carroll, Ill. The last four bulls are the present herd sires.

There has been an increased emphasis on showing at the local level since 1955. In the office are championship ribbons from the Mercer, Knox, Henry, Kane, Carroll, JoDaviess, Stephenson, Whiteside, Bureau, Rock Island, Winnebago, Tri-County at Mendota, and the Sandwich Fair Associations, ribbons or trophies for champion bull in the Illinois Association sale in 1954, champion female in 1953; from the Henry Co. Association sales two champion bulls and a champion heifer. The record for the top-price sold in the Association sales is held by an animal from the Abbott herd. The firm has been developing a market toward the sale of quality steer calves. In the past two years all but one calf (retained as a bull) of the spring and summer crop have been sold as club calves either at home or in auction sales in northern Illinois. The family is probably most proud of the set of silverplate, 1847 Rogers Bros., won in interbreed competition at Sandwich in 1965 for the best three females bred and owned by the exhibitor.

Some of the Abbott's registered Herefords graze in a bluegrass pasture across the highway from the homestead in 1962.

L.A. Abbott & Sons, Registered Herefords

Active Involvement

During the summer, the cattle thrive on fertilized permanent bluegrass pasture and in winter run in the stalk fields, with feedings of alfalfa hay, brome hay and silage when weather conditions limit the field forage. Water, salt and minerals are always available. For the six weeks prior to calving, each cow receives a daily ration of two pounds alfalfa hay purchased usually from New Melleray Abbey near Dubuque, Iowa. The personnel at the abbey carry on varied farm activities that include some superior beef cattle.

For the last five years, the Abbott herd has been one of six in the county on the Illinois performance testing program—a state-wide program to improve its beef breeding herds. All young breeding stock are performance tested twice a year, first for weaning weight and then for rate of gain. All heifers are vaccinated for Bangs and all animals for blackleg, malignant edema and hemorrhagic septicemia; all cows for leptospirosis. Within a few hours after being dropped, each calf receives a dose of terramycin, and if needed, a dose daily for the next two days to get it off to a good start.

Maintaining a registered purebred herd entails a good deal of book work and record keeping, ear tattooing and identification. To keep breed organizations strong and functioning requires active membership. L.A. Abbott is a former president of the Illinois Hereford Association, and Ed a former director of it. The firm is a member of the state association and the Henry County Hereford Association, which comprises the 17 northwest counties of Illinois. Ed is president of the Henry County association and among other activities is an elder in the Spring Valley Presbyterian Church, an assistant leader of the Union Grove Sod Busters 4-H club and a director of the Whiteside County Fair.

Big Old Don

Asked for an observation from a half century's association with Hereford cattle, L.A. Abbott says, "Some of the nicest folks I know are friends I made by way of the Herefords." Asked to recall some outstanding animal, he says, "Each animal is an individual just as a person is. Perhaps one we enjoyed the most was Donald Fairfax 3rd (931581), bought in 1927 from the University of Illinois.

L.A. Abbott & Sons, Registered Herefords

"In addition to his regular job as herd sire there he had 'worked his way through college' hauling the loaded manure carts out of the beef cattle barns each day for exercise. Big Old Don, as we nicknamed him, came to us with a confidence in the human race that endured to the end.

"Here, he was turned out with the cow herd and lived out his days in comfort. He had a magnificent set of horns that now hang in the office, a tribute to a great bull. Big Old Don would walk a mile for a scratch on the back and every person was a friend who might bestow it if only Don could get close enough.

"Late one summer afternoon we found him dozing under a tree in the timber patiently waiting for a terrified wild raspberry poacher to come down out of a tree and scratch him. The man still chattered with fright as he told from his perch how the big bull had come out of the bushes and chased him up a tree."

17. Corn Pickin' in the Good Old Days

October 1979

It's hard for today's farm children to visualize corn picking as it was done when their grandparents were their age. The huge picker-sheller today can level a 40-acre field in a day and have the shelled corn hauled in trucks to an elevator or river terminal miles away. Or it may take Dad a couple of days if he does the field with his big tractor and a 4- or 8-row picker and cribs the ear corn at home. And not a horse in sight as present-day yields of 100- to 200-plus bushels per acre are being harvested.

When Grandpa was a boy, harvesting the corn meant the pay-off on the year's work, just as it does now. Soybeans were not raised as a field crop here in any quantity until the 1930s, and corn was the principal grain crop. About this time of year, farmers selected seed for their next year's corn planting from their own fields, dried out during the winter on wire devices to be shelled and tested the next Spring to be certain of germination. Since then, hybrid seed corn has been developed and made available through the seed corn producers that has shortened the season and increased the per acre yield beyond the wildest dreams of the pioneer settlers. The field that could make 50 bushels an acre in 1920 now with proper management for 50 years, heavy commercial fertilizer application and favorable weather during the growing season can produce four or six times that much, and its potential is much more when an irrigation system is added.

Husking Pegs and Horses

Just as corn has changed, so has corn picking. Our earliest recollection of a husking peg—to pull back the husks from the ear—was handmade from a piece of wood about the size of a wooden clothes pin. It was whittled down to a fine point at one end and held in the palm of the right hand. How it was secured to the hand is vague, perhaps a little leather strap buckled over the back of the hand. But it satisfied the youngster who wanted to "help Dad."

All corn, even shocks in the field, was picked with husking pegs or hooks, or snapped. Pegs ranged from "kid size" to the deluxe store-bought models with wide leather bands to fasten around the hand and distribute the stress. Every man had his own favorite. Husking mittens were bought by the dozen, double thumb preferred, for around $1.50 to $2.00 a dozen depending on quality and thickness of material. Women of the family usually provided homeknit wristers to fill the gap between cuff of the mitten and the cuff of the shirt sleeve. Long corn leaves can be sharp and lacerating to exposed skin.

Next in importance to the men and their husking pegs were the horses and wagons. A good, quiet reliable team was essential—a team that could follow a row even if corn was down and tangled, a team that would amble along at a slow, steady pace or would start or stop on command with "Giddap" or "Whoa." Wagons must be readied for the month-long harvest, too, wheels greased, minor repairs here and there, the bangboards handy.

Most hired help picked by the bushel since few family farms had load-size scales. The standard wagon was 36 inches deep and an inch of corn was estimated to be a bushel. Thus a level wagon load was 36 bushels, with the width of each bangboard added as it was filled. The picker usually kept track of each day's work and the total was accepted by the owner.

A man usually could pick two or three loads a day when conditions were favorable—the corn standing good, yield good, a cooperative team, meals on time, and his turn to unload at the crib without waiting. Not many could average 100 bushels a day. Often the man was rated as a clean or dirty picker—clean if very few husks were left on the ears and dirty if many were visible in the crib.

Mechanical Pitfalls

One of the objections to the first mechanical pickers used in the area was the great number of husks left on the ears. Farmers just weren't used to having so many tell-tale husks flying from the slats of the cribs to indicate dirty picking. Another thing that "bugged" the

Corn Pickin' in the Good Old Days

early mechanical picker operator was a custom that went out after that first year. It was a common practice to raise the family's supply of squash and pumpkins along with the corn. The thrifty housewife saved the seeds from the best, and in the Spring as the loads of manure were hauled out and spread on the field to be planted in corn, she threw a generous handful of seeds on several loads to ensure a good supply of pumpkins and squash by fall. Usually enough seeds germinated, grew and survived cultivation. When the men picked by hand, the vegetables were spotted and put in the wagons to take home or were harvested later.

L.A. Abbott, about to unhitch a full wagon of picked corn on the south side of the Road, circa 1965.

After the first round was made by the mechanical picker, a little one-row machine, the decree went out—NO MORE squash or pumpkin seeds to be planted in a corn field! The picker just couldn't pick such juicy, big things, plugged, and refused to go again until the mess was cleaned out. Maybe a well-trained vine could be allowed on a fence, but no more in the field!

Corn Pickin' in the Good Old Days

And speaking of pumpkin pie—not all the corn crop was harvested on the ear. Along in September farmers who had silos would combine efforts and make up a run to exchange work. A silo-filling crew meant about fifteen or more men, some to cut the stalks in the field and load them on the hay racks as they were driven along; some unloading the bundles of stalks into the machine that cut the stalks and sent the silage up into the tall wooden silo, the man in the silo that led the distributor around, the machine operator—quite a knowledgeable crew, all hard workers who went from one farm to another until all the silos were filled. With good luck, the season lasted several weeks, but bad weather or mechanical breakdown sometimes kept a crew at one place for days. The housewife usually prepared breakfast for the machine men, served a lunch about 9:30 to the whole crew with basket lunch to the field men, had dinner on the table at noon and another lunch around 3:00 p.m.

By the end of the season, most women had exhausted their recipe files of a change of pies. Pie was the standard dessert as electricity had not reached this area. One woman, trying for a change from apple, pumpkin, cherry, peach, custard, raisin or coconut, remembered that the elderberries were just at their best and baked four elderberry/rhubarb beauties such as her family liked. Came noon and the crew washed up at the pump by the well and came in for dinner.

One young man looked over the dining table critically, pointed at the piece of pie on a plate and asked, "What kind of pie is that?" Thinking she had pleased him with a change, she replied, "Why, that's elderberry pie!" He sighed, sat down and said sadly, "I hoped it was blueberry. Of all the kinds of pies there are in the world, elderberry is the one kind I can't stand."

The Whole Family Helps

Corn picking by hand on most family farms was done by the family—Dad, the big boys, Mother and the big girls helping; the smaller ones on Saturdays, all trying to get the job done, the cribs filled and the cattle and hogs turned out to glean the fields before snow covered the ground. There were no dryers then and picking usually didn't start until late September. Thanksgiving Day was the target date for completion of the job, with a promise from Dad to take all the

- 50 -

small-fry rabbit hunting Thanksgiving morning if the corn was all out by that day.

Sometimes retired grandparents would return to the farm for the corn harvest to have the noon meal ready, which freed Mother so she could pick along with Dad, usually one row to his two rows. On Saturday, when children were not at school, even the youngest ones helped by picking up ears that were overlooked or had fallen short of the wagon. One of our friends recalls that on such a day as she and her sisters and brothers were picking along with their father, they complained that they were cold and wanted to go home. His reply was, "Work fast and you'll keep warm." So they did, until the load was full. They learned to work in spite of discomfort and honor him now for his good counsel, even though it seemed hard at the time, some 60 years ago.

Aunties, unworried by their own household responsibilities, seemed in greater supply in those days, especially the aunties gifted in cookie making. One remembers stirring up a double batch of those Melts-in-Your-Mouth, big, soft ginger cookies with sugar on top, after the noon meal dishes were done. By the time the men who were picking had come in for lunch, and the children coming home from school had found the cookies cooling on the kitchen table, there were not enough left for the next day's dinner pails for school.

A Pound of Meat A Day

A custom that went out with the advent of the mechanical picker reached into the animal department. Every farm had a faithful dog or two that felt duty-bound to accompany any team and wagon around the place, and going out in the early morning to pick corn meant a busy morning for Fido or Shep. They worked hard protecting the outfit from striped gophers and rabbits, chasing here and there for several hours. But by midmorning, when the sun had warmed a spot in the soft grass at the end of the field nearest the buildings, they curled up for a nap, but still alert, not to be left sleeping when the team went home for dinner. A dog just doesn't have the loyalty to a noisy big machine that it had for a team and a wagon.

For many years, corn picked by hand with pegs or hooks was unloaded by hand, a real chore for the men who had been picking from dawn to dark, perhaps a total of 100 bushels or more. The long day usually began around 5:00 a.m. for a hired man who went to the barn, fed, curried and harnessed his team. While the horses ate, he came in for a hearty breakfast of food enough to last until lunch or noon, depending on whether he was a "two-load or a three-load-a-day" man. Breakfast often included a hot cereal, pancakes or fried potatoes, eggs or meat, bread and butter, and plenty of coffee and milk. One farmer we knew didn't like to hire a man who couldn't eat at least a pound of meat a day.

After breakfast, the team was led out to the tank for water, then hitched to the corn wagon and the outfit rattled out to the field on the frozen ground to get the ears thumping against the bangboards, a sound that carried a mile in the frosty air before the sun was up.

Bringing in the load of 35-45 bushels, the unloading into the crib had to be staggered to accommodate the number of men picking. The corn was shoveled out of the wagon by hand and up maybe six to eight feet high—a real chore. Then a quick lunch or back to the field for another load, to come in for dinner around two o'clock, unload, and back for a third load by dark. A hearty supper around six or seven o'clock and then the dreaded job of unloading that last wagon by lantern light before going to bed. No wonder a man needed at least a pound of meat a day plus all the trimmings.

"Running The Board"

Then came welcome innovations—gas engines and later, electricity to power elevators, hoist and gravity wagons, drags, auxiliary elevators that eliminated some of the backbreaking shoveling and unloading. As mechanical pickers and elevators became more standard equipment, and farm laborers and horses disappeared from the scene, farm wives took on some of the duties of harvesting the crop. After a few lessons, most could manage the equipment and unload as fast as the wagons came in, and most enjoyed being able to help. Except for one phase of the job.

Most farmers seemed never content to have a crib filled to the top with the exception of bits of space at the far corners under the eaves. Filling those corners meant "Running The Board," which most women, after one trial, refused to do.

Unloading meant spotting the wagon so the corn would run out of a control into the drag which carried it along to the 30- to 40-foot

Corn Pickin' in the Good Old Days

elevator whose clattering metal chains and flights elevated it to the crib—all powered by electricity and a tractor, and all noisy. "Running The Board" meant standing in the upstairs of the long crib, rods away from the unloading process down below on the ground, and holding a wide board some 6- to 8-feet long at the proper angle for the ears that came thundering out of the elevator spout suspended from the ceiling to strike the board and be shot over into that far empty corner.

Mrs. Abbott avoids "Running The Board" by unloading a wagon of corn into the elevator on the ground during the 1962 harvest.

The person down below, slowly feeding corn into the drag, was alert for a signal from The Board holder to quit before everything was full. A first-time Board holder got along fine until all of a sudden, panic, panic, what to do? The corner is full, the corn keeps coming, The Board is too heavy to shift, corn piles up in the spout at the ceiling, the flights are full and the whole operation comes to a grinding halt. Why didn't she signal to stop sending it up? It takes a ladder and an hour to undo the mess an ear at a time!

Women have wondered about a solution to the problem—hide The Board? But there would be other boards. Start conditioning Dad's thinking early in the season that he'll have a pile of corn outside anyway so why try to squeeze a few more bushels into that corner? That won't work either so most women just refuse to RUN The Board and opt to do the unloading while Dad "Runs The Board" himself and can run to the far end of the crib and shout "Stop!" loud enough to be heard above the machinery.

That creates problems, too. One of our neighbors told of trying to signal to his wife to stop sending up any more corn but couldn't get her attention. So he threw down an ear of corn hoping it would land near her feet, but his aim was poor or the wind caught it and it hit the side of her head. Her reaction, as he reported it, "She quit, went to the house, and would scarcely speak to me for two days."

Maud and Topsy

We can't leave the era of horse-drawn machinery without a tribute to the fine animals that made a corn harvest possible.

Our favorite team was Maud and Topsy, a pair of beautiful, perfectly matched big, strawberry roan Belgians, perfect except that Topsy was blind. But Maud could follow a corn row for hours, even though the stalks were down and tangled. They had been owned for years by Roy Smaltz, who loved good horses. After his closing-out sale when he left the farm, the team lived here until they died of old age.

As they explored their new pasture we watched lest Topsy run into trouble. Maud led her slowly to the water tank, nudging her along, staying carefully between Topsy and the fence, and as they grazed never getting too far away from her blind friend. As they learned the new location, Maud amused herself by occasionally jumping over the fence, a trick she could do in the twinkling of an eye. One moment she was on one side of a fence, the next she was on the other side, but she never took advantage of her agility to stay on the wrong side.

Another of Maud's habits was to stall when led out of the barn to get a drink at the tank just before being hitched up for work. Topsy drank quickly, but Maud would stand sipping noisily and so slowly for minutes, knowing that as long as she seemed to be drinking she wouldn't be hitched up for work. They were a great team. Many pleasure horses are raised and enjoyed in the community, but few work horses are left. Probably few young persons could harness and hitch up a team now.

A Man's Word is his Bond

One method of harvesting the corn crop one seldom sees now was the tepee-like shocks in the fields, picturesque, with a cache of golden pumpkins almost hidden in them, safe from early frosts, immortalized by cartoonist John T. McCutcheon in his famous "Injun Summer." The shocks, built from stalks chopped off with a corn knife, later were hauled in as needed for the livestock, yielding not only corn ears but the fodder for roughage and bedding, plus the pumpkin pie material.

This always looked like an efficient system to utilize all the plant, but the manpower and time involved was discouraging. One man, remembering the not-so-good old days when corn shocks were considered good farming practice, came up with a way to balance state and federal budget. For every billion dollars a legislator or a congressman voted to budget annually, he should be required to dig and pry a frozen corn shock out of the snow and ice, load it on a wagon, sled or stone boat, haul it to the livestock, unload it and feed it. The idea never got out of committee. It might work now, if it could be enforced, but think of the bureaucracy it could create!

The wages for corn pickers has varied over the years along with the market price of corn and the per-acre yield. During the Depression years, pickers received two cents a bushel, plus room, board and laundry, or three cents if they lived at home. Gradually, the price rose to 15 cents per bushel before mechanical pickers eliminated hand picking.

After the 1929 crash, corn prices hit bottom and corn was used for fuel by some families who had no money to buy coal. Incredible, but it happened. During one of those hard years, our good neighbor, who had planted more corn than he estimated he would need for feed, watched the price going down, down, and when a cattle dealer from the Fulton area approached him in August about buying corn at harvest time, he agreed. They walked over the field in August and Jim agreed to sell it when harvested at 18 cents a bushel, with the buyer doing the picking. Hail, and then dry weather, cut the prospect of a good crop in the fall and the price went up to 40 cents a bushel delivered to an elevator.

A neighbor of the Fulton man came to Jim and said that he had heard he was selling corn for 18 cents that now was worth twice that much; that he was foolish and should raise the price or back out of the bargain. Without hesitation Jim replied, "No, sir. We walked through that cornfield in August and I made a deal with him for 18 cents a bushel which then seemed like a good price. The deal was 18 cents and that's what it's going to be even if corn goes to a dollar a bushel on the market." Jim Pearson was an honest man who believed a man's word should be as good as his bond, and lived that way.

Yields have varied from year to year, weather being a big factor. Lack of moisture (or too much), hail, a late Spring or early frost, have cut yields. In a few minutes, a hail storm has cut a beautiful field down to bare stalks, even the few remaining ears so damaged they lack nutritional value, which becomes evident in the livestock later on. In such a field, one farmer reported that he and his wife picked from early morning to mid-afternoon and got only enough nubbins for half a load.

For many years, the University of Illinois sponsored a 100-bushel corn yield contest with very few farmers producing that much per acre. Then came better farming practices. Limestone, fertilizers, soil analysis and hybrid seed now enable many to exceed 200-bushel-an-acre yields and are aiming at 300, with irrigation.

Ducking Duty

Not every farmer enjoyed corn picking, and stories of evasion of that job, that happened decades ago, still persist. A man who lived in the community then was a good farmer, got his crops in early in the spring but along in late August or September, after the small grain harvest, grew restless as corn picking neared and decided to take Horace Greeley's advice and "go West, young man, go West." Come October and he had not returned, his wife and children tried to begin the corn harvest but made little progress. As the neighbors finished, they went to help her get the crop in. About Thanksgiving time, the husband returned, full of stories of his adventures in the far West and thanked the neighbors for getting his cribs full.

Corn Pickin' in the Good Old Days

The next year the same thing happened, and the third year, until he seemed to expect to come home and find his work finished and began to be critical of the way the neighbors had done it. After small grain threshing the next summer his friends called on him and suggested he arrange his annual "vacation" at some other time or cancel it completely as they would not be picking his corn again—ever!

Another story is of a man who used another method of avoiding husking a corn crop. Farm neighbors always have been dependent on one another in times of sickness, accident or other trouble, just as they still are. This fellow feigned illness that kept him a bed patient, even convincing his wife as he writhed in pain, demanding almost constant care, even at night.

Hospitals were only in large cities, so neighbors volunteered to "sit up nights" with sick friends. Weary from a long day in the corn fields, the sitter in this story was established in a comfortable rocking chair beside the patient's bed where he could nap but still was available to wait on the sick man. Neighbors, sorry for the man's wife who was on duty all day, took turns as sitters at night.

Waking and finding the sick bed unoccupied, the sitter one night went in search of the patient and found him in the kitchen, apparently delirious, cold, shivering and in great pain. The sitters compared notes and found this happened often. So the next night, a sitter pretended to be asleep, snoring convincingly. The patient got out of bed, slipped on overalls, jacket and a pair of shoes and let himself out the back door. The sitter quietly followed him at a distance as he checked the cow barn, the horse barn, the hog house and the corncrib that was now nearly full of corn the neighbors had harvested, then turned toward the house.

The sitter had hurried back in to the house ahead of him and was snoring peacefully as the patient crawled into bed and, apparently in pain and having a chill, demanded a hot drink and a back rub. The sitter "awoke," told him what he had observed, that he now was going home, and "by morning, you'd better be well enough to start picking your own corn."

Corn Pickin' in the Good Old Days

Methods Have Changed

Now that the 1979 corn harvest is nearly completed, most of the long elevators are down and pickers and wagons are greased and put away until next fall, the varieties and numbers of the hybrids evaluated for next year's seed orders, and no corn shocks to bring in, we wonder what the future holds. Shall we be producing enough corn to power the machinery with gasohol? Then go full cycle with the old farm routine when after corn picking came working in the timber getting up the year's supply of wood to heat our homes, heat water and cook our food? After that came filling the farm ice house with chunks of ice sawed from the river after the Mississippi froze to a depth of a foot or so, enough to last well into the summer, layers separated by sawdust saved from wood sawing. Energy then didn't cost much money, just time and hard work. Methods may have changed, but not the men who accomplished so much.

18. Election Day a Civic, Social Event

November 1975

As usual, voters in Ustick took their privilege and responsibility to vote seriously with 86+ percent casting ballots between 6 a.m. and 7 p.m. at the town hall.

Including nine absentee ballots, 280 persons voted. Working on the election board were Mr. and Mrs. William Connelly, Mrs. Paul Zuidema, Mrs. Everett Bechtal and Mrs. L.A. Abbott.

Serving from 5 a.m. until all the "paper work" is finished at night and the returns safely delivered to the courthouse is a long day, but a pleasant one, with fringe benefits in addition to the compensation.

Early risers Nov. 4 saw the crescent moon and three planets closely grouped low in the eastern sky that morning, an arrangement the astronomers say will not occur again for many years.

The second fringe benefit continued all day, almost without interruption. How else could one see and visit a bit with 270 friends and neighbors, all in one day? Always there are stories of other elections—the year the Republican victory seemed so sure and a donkey pastured in the field adjoining the town hall lay down and died, but that omen was not reliable—the Democrats won.

Election boards in Ustick try to make elections attractive and begin early to entice young folks to vote and bring their parents. A bowl or two of candy, some cookies or other small goodies are passed to the children, and are available to the grownups, too. In fact, this year the only complaint of the day was from the man who thought the gumdrops were a bit too hard.

Election Day a Civic, Social Event

On very cold days, a cup of coffee may be offered to a man who came in from a long day in the field. But that works in reverse, too.

One nice day a housewife rode her bike two miles to the town hall to vote, accepted a cup of coffee but couldn't stay long because she had to hurry home to get the cinnamon rolls in the oven. In an hour or so, she was back with a big pan of warm cinnamon rolls, delicious as only homemade bread can be, for lunch for the election board. Where but a rural precinct would a busy woman pedal eight miles to give her neighbors such a treat?

Then there is the story from the "Good Old Days" when there were six on the election board instead of five as there are now. All were men, with the town supervisor always the chief judge responsible for the accuracy and honesty of an election.

Voting machines and punch card voting had not been dreamed of in those days. One simply wrote a name on a slip of paper or put his X in the square and dropped it in the ballot box.

The Supervisor, who was the chief judge that year, was a candidate for re-election but was being challenged by a man of the other party. During the day, the chief judge was observed scribbling on pieces of paper and dropping them in the ballot box. When the polls closed and the votes were counted there were 28 more votes cast than there were voters that day, and 28 pieces of paper with the chief judge's name in the same handwriting were declared illegal and void by the other five judges, who declared his opponent duly elected and so certified it to the county clerk.

The defeated chief judge tried to explain that he just hadn't realized what he was doing, just practicing writing his name to pass the time. In the Good Old Days, an election board could detect errors without challengers, affidavits or recounts, and usually justice was done.

19. Remember Armistice Day 1940?

November 1982

November 11, 1940, was still remembering the armistice that ended fighting in World War I, the war that would stop all wars and bring everlasting peace. Now we call it Veteran's Day, but we still honor and observe it.

November 11, 42 years ago, was a beautiful morning, as the whole Fall that year had been, and we started a big fire under the wash boiler for the routine Monday laundry for the family. Corn picking started at dawn, the first basket of clothes were on the line and drying in the warm breeze. Then the wind changed a bit and with each basketful the wind was stronger and colder. By the time the overalls were ready to hang out, they froze as we pinned them to the line.

The men came in for dinner before noon, ate a hasty meal, and put the teams in the barn. Instead of picking corn, and in spite of the strong and cold wind, climbed on the barn roof to nail down sheets of roofing that were being torn loose and blowing away.

That accomplished, they hurriedly drained radiators, hoses, sprayers, checked faucets and pumps. The wind had increased so one could scarcely stand against it and temperatures fell as the day wore on. Clouds were heavy and snow began about mid-afternoon. Chores were started early with an attempt to close all possible doors and windows against the wind. Chicken waterers froze in the henhouse and eggs froze in the nests.

The schedule for the day's work had changed in the house, too. Armloads of frozen clothing, stiff as boards and as unmanageable in the wind, had been brought in and stacked here and there to thaw.

The winter's supply of root crops—potatoes, carrots, beets, turnips—were still in the garden. Late cabbage and Chinese cabbage still grew there. A few Kiefer pears had been left to ripen on the tree. The Fall had been so warm and pleasant there had been no reason to bring things in too soon. Now it must all be done at once, but in what order?

Forget the pears, we had plenty in the house spread out to ripen. Better get the above-ground vegetables first—about 20 heads of cabbage to pull—were cabbages always so heavy? Five trips, with two in each hand, to the basement.

Then to dig or pull the root crops. By this time the ground was freezing, and instead of a fork to lift them out, a spade was needed. The vegetables were hastily thrown into a pail and taken to the basement—a setter can at a time—that seemed heavier with every trip. The ground froze as soon as exposed to the wind.

By the time the garden produce had been salvaged it was growing dark. Snow was driven by the wind into every crevice in the barns, where the men had concentrated on making livestock comfortable for the night.

We remember sitting on the bottom step of the basement stairs, too tired to get up. It had been a miserable day in every way. And there were still those wet, thawed-out clothes to do something with! So we climbed slowly up the stairs and got supper for the men, who were just as tired.

There had been no warning of a change in the weather pattern. We have since learned that the barometer that day registered 29.11, and the temperature 10 degrees with a 40 mph wind. No wonder we were cold, or that even now we're suspicious of Armistice Day, and glad when it has passed.

20. Moving Day

Undated

February has special days, Groundhog Day on the second, Lincoln's Birthday the 12th, Valentine's Day the 14th, that other patriot's birthday, Washington's on the 22nd, and every fourth year, Leap Year's Day on the 29th. Important as they may be, most farmers pay most attention to the first day of March which rates capital letters as Moving Day.

Most farm leases and many contracts run from March 1, a custom that has been followed for many years. Reasons are many; some have become obsolete as times change, others are more obvious than ever, and some developed because of weather patterns in various parts of the country.

March 1 in this latitude usually comes before the roads break up in the Spring when years ago a strong young team of mules would get stuck on hills trying to pull an empty wagon. It was advisable to get the hauling and moving done before the dirt roads thawed and wheels became balls of wet clay. Now with concrete, blacktop and good gravel roads, trucks and tractors, it wouldn't make as much difference for a man could move as much in an hour as he could have done in a day in the good old days.

One might ask why farmers don't do their moving, when changing farms, during the cold months when roads are frozen. The reason was, and is, that remaining on the farm where the crop is raised, until March 1, gives the man with livestock such as hogs, cattle, horses and sheep the opportunity to glean the fields during the fall and winter providing some four or five months of feed that would be lost in an early move. Hay and grain stored in barns or stacks is fed during the winter rather than having to be loaded and handled all over again during a move to the new location if he moved on January 1 or before.

Moving Day

The supply of foods stored for the family during the summer and fall for its winter use also was depleted by March 1. Empty fruit jars are easier to handle than full jars, and most of the fruits and vegetables such as apples, potatoes, squash, pumpkins, onions, carrots, turnips, beets and cabbage had been carried up from the cellar and made into tasty meals before Spring.

His Fair Share

Cattle and hogs had been fed the grain and roughage and many had gone to market, which simplified settlement between landlord and tenant if the lease was on a share basis or provided the money if on a cash basis. Division of the breeding livestock remaining sometimes created problems that were solved in various ways. If either landlord or tenant expressed a desire to buy the other's half and could agree on the price it was simple, or an appraiser might be enlisted to determine their value, which could be accepted or rejected. Sometimes a public sale was necessary to satisfy both.

Occasionally both men were willing to draw lots for the first choice of animals and alternate choices were then made, which usually proved satisfactory. With this system, the tenant who had worked with the animals, particularly with the dairy cows and knew their individual worth and potential far better than the landlord did, had the advantage. The disadvantage of this system was that the cattle had to be separated one by one or ear tags noted as choices were made.

One tenant, hoping to outsmart the landlord told him that to make the division as simple as possible—since all the milk cows were of equal quality—he just tied them all in a row of stanchions in the barn and thus could easily load up his half, which would leave the other half safe in the barn. His idea was that the landlord would agree and probably suggest that the tenant might as well take the half that was tied nearest the door for easy loading. However, the landlord knew the tenant's propensity for sharp dealing, and looked the cattle over and said he would choose the half nearest the door even though he would have to move them elsewhere before the half left for the tenant could be loaded. The tenant protested the extra work involved, knowing full well he had put the best cattle nearest the door expecting them to be his share.

Moving Day

All sharp dealing wasn't on a tenant's side; some landlords demanded what seemed a more than accurate accounting on a share basis. Years ago, some high-concentrate feeds for young animals were sold in 100-lb. cloth bags, and some in bags with a 'premium,' usually a dish suitable for table use to encourage use of that particular brand until a set of dishes could be acquired. The cloth bags came in many colors and patterns and were used to make dresses, aprons, toddler's clothes, curtains, drapes and quilts.

Obliging dealers would let the housewife choose the bags of feed until she had enough material of one pattern for the article she was making. It seemed that often that particular bag would be the bottom one of a big pile of sacks. One landlord earned a miserly reputation demanding his half of the dishes and the feed sacks that had been the premiums collected during those Depression years with the sacks of feed necessary for the young animals.

Weeks of Planning

With March 1 the target date for the shift of the farm population of a community, it was necessary for it to be accomplished in an orderly manner, one after another in succession as a row of dominoes set on edge might tumble down. If by some arrangement a family could move a few weeks before that date, it simplified things all down the line. Or if, by agreement, machinery and most of the hay stacks could be moved to the new location while roads were solid that helped. However, some tenants and landlords would not allow the new family to come before the first of March, nor the old tenant to move out and leave the premises unoccupied.

Moving Day meant a great deal of planning weeks before. Neighbors with teams and wagons, willing hands and strong backs offered or were asked to help. Arrangements were made for babies and pre-schoolers to be left with relatives for the day. It seemed there were a million things to think of outside and inside the house. Chickens were moved at night, if possible, lifted quietly from their roosts, put into crates borrowed from a Produce House or into sacks and boxes and taken to the new location lest the laying pattern of the flighty fowl be disrupted—all depending whether or not the henhouse at the new location had been emptied. The family dog usually went along with the family and the children were sure to insist on a favorite cat or two being included.

Family and neighbors turned out to help farmers move on March 1, as households packed up everything, heading up the road to better prospects.

Good Housekeepers

The homemaker of a moving family had problems, too. Breakables had to be packed ahead of time for bouncing over the roads in wagons, canned goods and vegetables carried up from the cellar, curtains washed and stretched ready to hang at the new home, bedding all laundered, clothes clean, since laundering was easier than it might be after moving. Food for school lunches, meals and lunches for the family, neighbors and relatives who might be helping must be plentiful

Moving Day

and easy to reheat and serve, the most-used housekeeping equipment as handy as possible.

Some homemakers who wished to maintain a reputation as "good housekeepers" would have all the woodwork and washable walls washed, as well as windows washed several weeks ahead of time in the house they were leaving, and would arrange with neighbors or relatives to scrub the floors as each room, upstairs and down, was emptied on Moving Day. Clean papers were then laid down on the floors, so as the new tenants moved in, the floors were not soiled. From cellar to attic, the new tenants came to a clean house.

Unfortunately, not all homemakers were good housekeepers. When Moving Day came they simply left and the farm woman replacement had to begin Spring housecleaning before she could get supper that evening. Usually several of her farmer neighbors came along and helped her get established—sweep, dust, scrub, set up beds, find dishes, pots and pans enough to get a meal on the table.

Cattle Drive

Depending on the distance to the new place, the cattle and other livestock were driven on foot or hauled in wagons, before the days of livestock trucks and trailers. Most fields and yards were fenced at that time but when a herd of cattle was to be driven, several outriders on horseback preceded them to prevent them trying out every open gate, lane and road. After the initial friskiness, as the animals started after confinement in a feed yard, they usually behaved well, except an occasional bull who seemed to resent the change.

One supposedly gentle bull being led behind a buggy planted his feet firmly, put his head under the vehicle and tossed it and the driver into the ditch. Another with a mean disposition was to be sent to market and was being delivered to the stockyards for rail shipment to slaughter in Chicago. The easiest method was to include such an animal with a few gentle cows that would follow the road as men on horseback escorted them to the stockyards several miles away. Once he was safely inside the corral, the patient cows were sorted out and driven back home.

Such a herd started out early one morning and enroute came in sight of a rural one-room schoolhouse with an unfenced yard. An alert farm boy, knowing the ways of cattle, rushed into the schoolhouse and reported to the teacher that there was a great big bull in the lead, pawing and bellowing. She called all the children in from the playground and shut the doors, just in time. The bull had seen the activity in the schoolyard as something to vent his temper on, menacingly circled the schoolhouse several times until the men got him back on the road.

Chores at the new farm were hard for a few days until the livestock became accustomed to different yards, pastures, barns, stanchions and routine.

"Three Moves are as Bad as a Fire"

While the work of moving all a family's possessions except household things could be spread over several weeks with mutual agreement of landlord, tenant and the owner and tenant at the other end, moving the family and all their household goods had to be accomplished in a single day. The mother had been working at it for weeks, sorting, packing, discarding; hoping for a warm, dry day on March 1.

The night before the big day, a neighbor would back up his wagon to the back door. After an early breakfast, and as soon as the big cook stove had cooled enough to be handled, it was loaded along with kindling and fuel onto this wagon, which would be the first to go. The horses were hitched to the wagon, which had the makings of a dinner to be ready as soon as the other wagons arrived with the remainder of the household furnishings.

Often the homemaker remained at home to supervise loading and a relative—grandma, aunt, mother or sister—went with that "chuck wagon" load to see that the stove was set up properly, the fire going to warm the house, plenty of hot coffee ready for the first arrivals, and a hot dinner ready to put on the table for 10 or 15 hungry men as soon as the chairs were set in place.

As the other loads came, furniture was set in place, beds put together and made up for the night, the heating stove unloaded and started, fuel brought in for the woodbox. Women helping laid clean papers on the pantry and cupboard shelves and were putting dishes, pots and pans away. The family dog wandered around, overjoyed when neighbors brought the children from the "old school," and by sundown and a late supper the family was pretty well established in the new home. Always a few things couldn't be found, a few were broken, mislaid or lost—as one man observed who had moved many times, "Three moves are as bad as a fire."

Why then did farmers move? Usually it was an attempt to better themselves—a better farm, a bigger farm, or the lifetime ambition to own their own farm finally achieved. March 1 was a day for a new beginning, a chance to make new friends and to prove there are good neighbors everywhere.

21. Maybe Old July 4th Celebrations Were Best

July 1979

It's nice to be old enough to remember the days before automobiles and gas shortages were important to the celebration of the Fourth of July; when homemade ice cream for dinner, a few fire crackers and a piece of punk to light kept the kids busy in the afternoon, and a couple of pinwheels to light after dark was a spectacular fireworks display!

Even these simple ingredients for a proper celebration required thought and effort. A cake of ice was dug out of the sawdust, washed off and chipped to the proper size to use in the hand-turned wooden freezer, while the mother of the family prepared custard with fresh farm eggs and real cream. Everyone took a turn cranking the handle as the salt melted the ice and the custard became "slushy." More ice and more salt were added from time to time, the handle was turned for what seemed a very long time, until at last it would go no more and the ice cream was pronounced "done."

The dasher was removed and awarded to the youngest children, who were standing by, armed with spoons to lick it clean. The freezer then was properly packed with ice and salt and the whole thing covered with a blanket to let it "ripen and harden," to be at its best by dinner time.

The firecracker supply took a bit more doing ahead of time. There were odd jobs to earn a few pennies, maybe a nickel or two, after school was out for the summer.

The Rags, Old Iron Man always was a source of money, and kids picked up nails and pieces of old scrap iron around the place; the girls of the family usually had an old gunny sack of rags ready for him when he made his periodic visits.

Then the trip to the store, where bunches of firecrackers were sold for a nickel with a piece of punk "thrown in," and a small skyrocket one could fasten to a fence post and a pinwheel to whirl after dark each cost a few cents more. For a quarter, one could really celebrate properly, and if several families could combine efforts, what a wonderful display it was!

The Fourth was a bad day for the dogs of the neighborhood. Some early riser usually set off a firecracker about daylight. The big boys, who were brave, were allowed to light a cracker under an empty tin can and then run for cover before the explosion, which put the dogs under porches or under the bushes for the day. Everybody had to try a sizzler, made by breaking a cracker part way through, and then igniting the exposed powder.

For the families who lived in town, the celebration was different. Most small towns, as well as the bigger ones, had their own ways of celebrating Independence Day.

Perhaps there were booths set up on Main Street, with bunting decorating the store fronts and flags waving from the windows. A parade was made up of floats of various kinds, with firehouse volunteers pulling the hose cart; the delivery wagons had a place, too. Kids asked weeks before for the privilege of riding one of the delivery horses. There were still Old Soldiers from the Civil War, given places of honor in carriages. The band played—it was wonderful. Usually there was a program, and sometimes a ballgame.

So who needs an automobile and a tank of gas to drive a couple hundred miles to celebrate the Fourth of July? Maybe we're overlooking something.

22. One-Room Schools Host Corn Carnivals

January 1980

Stories of corn picking in the early days bring to mind memories of the Corn Carnivals that many who attended country schools in Whiteside County in the first quarter of this century may remember. Ustick Township, being strictly rural, is a good example to use for this story.

One-room schools were established in Ustick Township from 1841 to 1871. Land for sites was given for that purpose by a farmer, or bought for a token price. Locations were chosen, as much as possible, to accommodate the families, so children were within walking distance of not more than two miles from a schoolhouse. Ustick is one of Whiteside County's few square, 36-section townships, and in a 30-year period was divided into eight school districts all different in size, shape, soil type and population, but conforming pretty well to the two-mile rule of thumb.

Names of the eight districts were interesting. Cottonwood was so named because the lumber for the first school building in that district was obtained from those trees on an island in the Mississippi River, hauled by ox team to a sawmill at Unionville. Spring Valley was a descriptive name, very appropriate to the area.

Otter Bluff, where the first school in the township was held in 1841 in the upper room of the Amos Short cabin, was built against the bluff at the edge of the Mississippi River bottoms where trapping was an early and lucrative business, and otters were abundant.

The Crouch School was named for the Crouch family who gave the land for the site of the school. The Robertson School, the

One-Room Schools Host Corn Carnivals

Cobb School and the Gridley School also were named for the early families active in establishing schools in their neighborhoods.

The Goff School, last of the eight districts created, also carried the name of an early family, although the land needed was given by James G. Gridley, who also had given the land necessary for the Gridley School.

The year of the first of the Corn Carnivals is uncertain, but when H.B. Price, who had been superintendent of the Fulton schools for some years, was elected County Superintendent of Schools and assumed that office about 1915, Corn Carnivals were encouraged and became popular.

Host Privileges, Duties Rotated

Teachers of a township usually met in early September and chose a Saturday agreeable to Mr. Price, who attended each Corn Carnival in the county and presented an American Flag to the school earning the most points in the day's activities. Since not many Saturdays were available before cold weather for such outdoor activities, competition was keen for an early booking.

Actually, a Corn Carnival was a mini-fair, a county fair on a township scale that lasted only a day with entries limited to the schools in that township vying with one another for the honors. Corn was stressed—best ear, longest ear, tallest stalk, corn of different colors. Also entered were vegetables, flowers, samples of penmanship, freehand drawing, maps, arts and crafts done by the pupils. A program of races included a school directors' race, teachers' race, three-legged race, sack race, boys and girls races for various ages, a ball game and other contests as time permitted.

Privilege of hosting the yearly event rotated among the districts because, in most townships, all had similar, limited facilities; preference always was expressed for schools toward the center of the township. The trip to the Big Day often was made with pupils and teacher riding on a hayrack with real horse power.

Hosting the Corn Carnival meant extra work for the teacher, pupils and directors. The yard, supposedly well mowed like a hay field before school opened that fall, would be hand raked, perhaps lawn mowed close to the building, and all trash removed in a general "sprucing up."

One-Room Schools Host Corn Carnivals

Inside the schoolhouse, probably freshly cleaned or painted for the opening of school, the kerosene lamps would be polished again, floors, desks and other furniture dusted, desks cleared of extra things, books in straight rows, windows washed; even the basement if there was one, came in for a housecleaning. Blackboards were washed, erasers clapped, and wall spaces assigned to show the various exhibits. Table and shelf space was cleared for baking, sewing, garden and field exhibits. First-graders often made dainty curtains of daisy chains for the windows.

Belief in Home Rule

Affairs of a rural school district were the responsibility of the three directors elected each Spring by the legal voters of that district. To them fell the tasks of hiring a teacher, maintaining the building and grounds, financial problems, and all the major and minor problems that might arise in such a job. If the furnace or stove smoked, the pump didn't work, the lock on the door stuck, a window got broken, the broom wore out, the teacher became ill or quit, a tree was needed for the Christmas program, the Railroad paid its taxes under protest—these and many more became the directors' problems.

Rural folks believed in home rule in education, and having accepted the office of school director, would cooperate as needed to make their school succeed.

So when Corn Carnival day rolled 'round, if transportation was needed such as a hayrack or team and driver or several Model Ts, depending on enrollment, the teacher would appeal to the directors and it would be provided. Going by hayrack always was more fun for everybody.

The Big Day: Food, Games, Prizes

Arriving at the host school about mid-morning with the entries of pupils' school work, the teachers carefully arranged them on walls and blackboards for the judges' later inspection. Meanwhile, the older boys and girls were entering their efforts—ears of corn, tallest stalks, vegetables, flowers, candy, baking, sewing and such items while the younger pupils tried out at teeter-totter, played ball, and got acquainted with others who were arriving.

One-Room Schools Host Corn Carnivals

About noon, parents and friends came with picnic baskets and each district spread its dinner on the grass, in sunshine on a cool day or in shade if the day were warm, with seats from the cars (cushions were removable in those days) for those who chose not to sit on the ground. Along with the good food, neighbors shared opinions on harvest prospects, swapped recipes and visited until time for the afternoon activities to begin.

While the athletic program was in progress, judging of the entries inside the building was done by disinterested men and women from outside the area. Members of an active Household Science Club in Morrison would provide several women to help. Farm Bureau was just getting started in Whiteside County and Farm Adviser L.O. Wise and his assistant, George Thiem, along with Farmers' Institute members John Martin and A.N. Abbott, helped judge the garden and field entries.

Playgrounds and other recreational programs were beginning to be stressed in towns and cities, and a group of businessmen from Clinton seemed willing to come to Corn Carnivals to supervise the afternoon games and races. The name of Bill Jacobsen comes to mind as being helpful in bringing several other men to act as starters, time keepers and judges (with real stop watches!) and to tabulate the results.

There were high jumps, broad jumps, shot puts, even a horseshoe game. Races included the teachers' race in which one or more, unaccustomed to such exercise, fell down to the amusement of the gallery of grownups who had carried the car seats and the recitation benches from the schoolhouse to vantage points in the yard. Casualties were frequent in the three-legged race, the sack race, the relay races for various ages of boys and girls, but entrants in the directors' race usually crossed the finish line in good form.

Little folks enjoyed a peanut scramble and, if time permitted, a ballgame might be organized while teachers, pupils and parents waited for the final count of points won in the games and entries, and the coveted Flag was presented to the winning school by the County Superintendent of Schools.

Entries on exhibit inside the building then were viewed by all, judges' decisions were discussed and the award ribbons proudly collected. Teachers rounded up their charges with their entries and the hayracks and carloads of farm folks went home to start chores—

everybody tired but happy to have had a day off to spend with their neighbors. The Flag went home with the winning school, where it would be displayed proudly, proof that a district that works together can win.

Weather No Obstacle

Remembering Corn Carnival days with several friends who were pupils or teachers in those days brought memories of other townships' observances. Just in case the day was rainy, as seldom happened in Indian summer season, some provision was made for indoor activities.

Colored chalk was handy for blackboard freehand competition, colored construction paper and scissors for freehand silhouette cutting and mounting, lists ready for spelldowns for each grade and the adults, guessing games and puzzles. Each school was encouraged to have ready at least one number for an impromptu program indoors if the weather didn't improve.

In the event of rain, Corn Carnivals were seldom cancelled. Some schools elected not to come, and those who did come enjoyed the day as best they could. Especially remembered was the picnic dinner, served inside, districts not separated but dining as a township with boundaries forgotten as the fried chicken, potato salad, cakes and coffee were passed around.

Two Fine Educators

Another friend, a native of Garden Plain Township, thinks that H.B. Price, County Superintendent of Schools in 1914, did not initiate Corn Carnivals, but that his predecessor, B.F. Hendricks, did instead. She says, "I was a pupil at Garden Plain then, before 1914, and for at least two years Cedar Creek, East Clinton, Lockhart and Mt. Hope, among others, came to Garden Plain, but then it was on a 'school day,' not a Saturday. It probably was bigger and better under Mr. Price. I seem to remember best the evening entertainment after the day of outside contests in the chilly air; once, we had a box social."

Memories of the two County Superintendents surface also. One remembered as follows—"My recollection from school days of Mr. Hendricks is not in connection with Corn Carnivals. It was his custom to visit each of the more than 100 rural schools in the county at least once each year, the trip being made in a top buggy pulled by a gentle bay horse. It stood tied to a fence post, dozing, while Mr. Hendricks paid his annual visit, which lasted about an hour.

"Teachers and pupils were on their best behavior, and he always praised them for good recitations and neat work. One custom he never forgot was to designate one child to have a 'piece' memorized to speak for him in his next visit. I still remember a few lines of the piece in our language book I learned the week after his visit, and rehearsed for a year, almost dreading his next visit, yet pleased to be chosen.

"Mr. Price also visited each school at least once a year, driving a Model T Ford instead of a horse and buggy. We looked forward to his visits because he always told us about the early history of our particular community and pointed out the important things and places of our township and district—such as the Mississippi River we always have taken so for granted, and the fact that we could stand on the bluffs and see clear over to Iowa, just as the Indians did years before the French explorers found the river. Not a pupil in the county but benefited from knowing those two fine educators."

23. Snowstorms Bring Out Angels, Tobogganners

January 1982

Snow seems to have lost the charm it had some decades ago. No one had heard of "Snow Days" when schools closed. Everyone bundled up with long underwear, leggings over the long wool stockings, and overshoes and walked to school. Drifts were a challenge that should be waded through to test their depth. Fluffy new snow meant lying down carefully, then flailing the arms to create angel wings for one's imprint to see who could make the prettiest angel. And if Teacher permitted, the water bucket could be used to make an icy slide in the school yard.

The first big boy or girl to arrive at the school after a snowstorm usually laid out a big Fox and Goose ring before too many tracks spoiled its outline. To make a really challenging ring, a concentric circle was added with connecting paths. If the setup proved too difficult to catch a goose, two "Its" were chosen for this game of tag. On an icy surface, Crack the Whip could keep everyone warm, too.

Some 65 to 70 years ago, coasting and tobogganing were favorite winter sports in Fulton. Automobiles were no problem, since most cars were jacked up in the corncrib or barn for the winter; antifreeze hadn't been invented and radiators froze. With the added chore of starting a cold car by hand cranking, most folks either walked to where they wanted to go or stayed home, and hills were safe for coasting.

There were several good coasting hills; favorite of the small fry was the Ninth Street hill from as far up as one's folks said it was safe to go, or from the very top beyond the High School. It had a nice, undulating course with a sort of breakwater at every crossing; with a good start, a one- or two-passenger sled might get as far as three blocks.

For the teenagers, the Cherry Street hill (now Tenth Avenue) was the favorite. All kinds of sleds and toboggans came out of storage after a good storm. Several big boys had toboggans that would carry eight or 10, depending on size. Loaded at the crest of the hill between what are now Eighth and Ninth Streets, with two husky pushers who could jump on at the last minute, away we went, not slowing down for side streets, across Main Street, across the Q rail tacks, and with good luck, a few feet more.

Then pull the toboggan back up the hill and do it over again—so tired by the time the Q passenger train was due it was time to quit and go home. Mr. Plunkett, who tended the tower, probably would have sent the kids home anyway. As the Indian described tobogganing: "WHOOSH—walk a mile!"

Heavy snow brings light traffic on the Lincoln Highway in the 1950s. The Pines was named for the six White Pine trees planted by the six Abbott brothers in 1902, as a memorial to their mother.

24. Christmases Past

December 1982

Looking back to the Good Old Days some decades ago, Christmas was much more simple than today when commercial radio and television influence thinking. Two characters stand out in earliest recollection—Jesus and Santa Claus.

Jesus was a baby with loving parents Joseph and Mary to look after him, and God took care of everything. No problem there. Santa Claus lived at the North Pole with Mrs. Claus who kept a flock of elves busy all year making presents for good boys and girls. No problem there, no conflicts of interest, everybody loved babies and everybody loved Santa Claus.

Because God gave us Jesus, the teacher of the Beginners' Class told us, we should give gifts of love to others, and helped with a solution to the problem. Before the days of electric razors, fathers lathered faces with soap, shaved with straight razors, and used paper to wipe the blades. The standard gift was a supply of newspaper sheet about a foot square threaded on a string to hang near the sink. A plain piece of white paper with a holly wreath crayoned on it covered father's gift. For mother, the crayoned picture of a Christmas tree loaded with colored packages was a loving gift any child could create with a little help.

By the time we started to school, we knew the Christmas songs "Away in a Manger," "Silent Night," and "O, Tannenbaum" that were sung in Sunday School and church. A program involving every child was given before Christmas, usually on Christmas Eve. Pieces to speak, dialogues, acrostics, songs, all had been memorized and rehearsed many times so the performance went smoothly. Standing in a corner at the front of the sanctuary would be a tall Christmas tree, probably a native red cedar, decorated with strings of popcorn and cranberries, ropes of tinsel and homemade ornaments.

Christmases Past

Small, real wax or tallow candles in little tin clip-on holders were clamped to the branches and lighted for the finale of the evening—the noisy entrance of Santa Claus through the front door. The jingle of sleigh bells and a stamping of feet heralded his arrival, which proved to half-hearted believers that he really did come with sleigh and reindeer.

Each Sunday School teacher had a wrapped small gift for each child in his/her class, and in return received an inexpensive gift from each, or perhaps a group gift arranged by mothers of the class. Any dedicated teacher, who over a lifetime had several generations of children in her class, probably had put away dozens of crochet- and tatting-trimmed hankies "too good to use."

In some churches, each child in the Sunday School and also in the audience received a small box of candy and nuts provided by the church. A few families brought individual gifts for their own children for Santa to distribute from the tree before he left—a practice frowned on by some because it tended to disappoint those children who received nothing extra, and could create jealousy and friction.

As the evening wore on and the tree's fragrance was released in the warmth near the ceiling, the little wax candles became soft and folded over, still lighted. Miraculously, they burned themselves out and a dipper of water from the bucket of water placed near the tree for an emergency never was needed.

Always it had been a lovely evening. The children's voices in the hymns could well have been an angel choir, the baby Jesus was beloved and would be the power to overcome evil on the earth. The three big boys in borrowed long bathrobes, shepherd's crooks in hand, played their parts well, the wise men in oriental garb had presented their gifts. The soloists and piece speakers hadn't needed prompting. The big night of the year was a success.

There was such a feeling of well being as we hurried home in the frosty air, a light dusting of snow making all creation beautiful, catching the cheerful glow of hardcoal burning heating stoves in the homes of friends along the way, wondering if Santa Claus really would bring that warm fur muff we had requested in a letter.

Santa already had been there and we missed him! A tree, beautifully decorated was in the parlor and packages were under it to be opened on Christmas Day. How busy those wives had been to get something like this ready for every home!

One stocking per child was hung on a chair by the tree—only one, never two—that would have been selfish. In the toe, in the morning, before integration and ecumenical were commonly used words, was a nigger toe (Brazil Nut), to indicate that Santa Claus loved every child, black or white, and didn't care whether little black toes or white toes would wear that stocking. In the leg of the stocking was an apple, an orange, a shiny new pencil and a pair of mittens. But no muff. Oh, well, with so many children wanting so many things, Mrs. Claus and the elves probably got names and addresses mixed up or ran out of time. The mittens would be warm enough.

Planning in October for the Christmas program in late December may not produce the desired results as any Sunday School teacher will agree. A Christmas Eve program given many years ago in a Morrison church may be remembered by some Old Timers. Considerable planning had gone into the effort to have a really good and meaningful program, well-rehearsed and costumed as authentically as possible. But a week before the scheduled date, snow piled up in drifts, followed by bitterly cold weather that touched off an epidemic of colds and flu. After-school rehearsals were cut short, cast substitutions were necessary; some numbers were shortened or deleted.

On the appointed evening, attendance was good and the program was given as completely as possible, but pastor and teachers who had hoped to have an outstanding presentation were disappointed. At the conclusion, the pastor enumerated the difficulties they had encountered. Thinking that some child who had had a part before becoming ill, might still wish to perform and was present, he asked that anyone who had a piece to speak and had not been called on, to please come to the platform and do so.

In those days, the Chicago and Northwestern Railroad still ran passenger trains from Chicago to Morrison and beyond. A family from Downers Grove arrived on the early evening train to spend the holiday with Grandma and went directly to the church for the program.

Little Dottie, age about four, seated between her mother and grandmother, heeded the pastor's plea for help with the program, scrambled over the adults' feet, raced up the aisle and onto the stage.

Christmases Past

There she made a polite low bow and proclaimed in a clear voice that carried to every corner:

"I asked my Mother for fifty cents
To see the elephant jump the fence.
He jumped so high
He reached the sky
And never came back
'Til the Fourth of July."

She curtsied and ran back to her embarrassed adults, certain that she had been obedient and helpful and would be in good standing with Santa Claus.

25. School Christmas Programs

January 1983

In the Good Old Days, transportation problems often prevented country children from taking an active part in Christmas programs in churches in town which their families attended on Sundays and for mid-week prayer meetings.

But the one-room rural school more than made up for this as a teacher had practically a captive cast to work with all day—before school, during recesses, at noon, and after school. Every district was assured an excellent program with every child involved.

A lack of electricity ruled out some things, but the tree would be tall. Usually it was a native cedar that had grown in some fence corner sheltered from livestock, observed for several years as "a nice tree for our school." It would be cut, delivered and set up touching the ceiling by the school directors, the week before the program. Little wax candles in clamp-on tin holders provided lights that then seemed wonderful.

For weeks, the smallest kindergarten-age pupils had been making daisy chains of colored paper. Those with tinsel ropes were looped lovingly across the big tree, strings of popcorn and homemade decorations were added, as well as donated shiny ornaments sent from home. Daisy chains hung at the windows like drapes or curtains gave a homelike look to the big room.

The kerosene lamps in the wall brackets were filled and the glass chimneys washed and shined, ready to light. Aladdin lamps were the coming thing then. If the program was to be at night, several families known to have them would be asked for their use. To be transported outdoors, the mantles must be lighted at home and somehow sheltered from wind or moisture or they disintegrated and blew away if the light went out. But they were wonderful if they worked properly and pressure was maintained with a small pump.

A Farm and Barn By the Side of a Road

Teacher Dorothy Sharer welcomes the last class of students to the one-room Cottonwood School in 1958. From left: Elwyn Newendyke, Timmy Valk, Kathy Smith, Karen Wray, Joyce Seifken, Cheryl Ottens, Janice Newendyke, Lawana Smith, Sandra Snyder, Patricia Daniels, Kathleen Valk, John Tervelt, Allen Ottens, Mrs. Sharer, Edwin Snyder and Arnold Snyder. Absent: Gary Jones.

A daytime program was easier but attendance was less as fathers and big brothers might have work at home that had to be done during daylight hours before winter arrived to stay.

Music for such school events depended on teacher's ability as organist or pianist, if the district was affluent and had such a luxury, or on an older girl or on a mother who had talent and enough time to come in for practices with the pupils.

Usually, a program consisted of pieces, dialogues (not always religious, some were downright slapstick comedy), acrostics with big pasteboard letters or figures, and all performed beside the big tree that sometimes crowded things a bit. Santa always arrived in costume to pass out the candy treats and small gifts provided by the teacher, and to present teacher's gifts that varied from family to family but were always welcomed enthusiastically.

26. A Farm and Barn By the Side of a Road

Circa 1976

One of Ustick Township's oldest landmarks is gone, and remnants of the huge, old barn on the Robert Merema farm on Millard Road will be used in ways its builder and first owner never thought of. Dimensions of the barn were approximately 115 feet long, 60 feet wide and 35 feet high to the hay track in the center, to allow for 200 tons of loose hay between the horse stalls for 16 horses on the east side, and stanchions and shed room for cows and cattle to the west. Loads of hay entered from the north between the horse barn and the hayloft, and were unloaded with horses and a hay fork.

Three generations of the Crouch family have owned the farm and the barn, which was built about the late 1880s or early 1890s as nearly as can be learned, since no descendents of the Crouchs remain. Mrs. Everett Bechtel, whose late father, Arthur C. McKee, was administrator of the estate of Dwight M. Crouch, third owner, who died in 1950, supplies information from records of the pioneer family.

Ashbel C. Crouch, 1814-1901, of English ancestry, for 40 acres paid $100.00 to J. Gordon Hewitt, Jr., of the County of New York and State of New York, for which a warranty deed was filed June 20, 1864, for the S.W. ¼ of the S.E. ¼ of Sec. 17, twp. 22 R. 4, E. of the 4th P.M. Ustick Township. By 1853, 160 acres in Sec. 20 are listed and total taxes that year were $2.85--$1.76 for real estate and $1.09 for personal property.

Present owners of the farm, Mr. and Mrs. Robert Merema supply additional information. An entry Mar. 31, 1854, in the Land Book of Whiteside County lists 80 acres to A.C. Crouch and A. Bolick, and also the patent dated Sept. 15, 1854 and filed Aug. 31,

A Farm and Barn By the Side of a Road

1861, book 17, page 276, the United States to Ashbel C. Crouch and Amos Bolick. Bradstreet Robinson of Fulton held a mortgage of $1,200.00 plus interest on it from 1870 to 1877. W.C. Snyder of Fulton claims to have had a tax title to a portion of it.

At Ashbel's death in 1901, the property passed to his only living son, Melvin D. Crouch, 1858-1940. The year before the latter's death he signed a receipt of balance of full purchase price of the 200 acres in the "home place" to his only son, Dwight M. Crouch, who operated it until his death in 1950.

It was owned next, in 1953, by George Balk who sold it in 1958 to the Meremas for $400.00 an acre. They since have added two 80-acre tracts—one from the adjoining Lahey farm and one from the S.J. Akker farm.

The Big Barn

Ashbel, builder of the big barn, is said to have used the best grade of lumber, which he obtained for $16.00 per thousand feet, for the framework, from the Lamb sawmill in Clinton. The top carpenter was paid $2.00 per day, the other carpenters less. Men who worked in the sawmill then received ten cents an hour for a ten-hour day. So long was the barn roof only four rows of wooden shingles could be laid in a day. A stairway and handmade ladder reached into the hay loft and the floored second story from either side. Square nails were used as well as wooden pegs, and floors were made of heavy plank.

Credit for the above paragraph goes to Henry Buikema, of Morrison, who as a boy often played in the barn with his schoolmate, Dwight Crouch. Henry's father, John Buikema, had worked for Melvin, rented land from him and later bought the farm Melvin owned east of the Crouch place at the end of a lane that ran north to land owned by Melvin and tenanted by a brother-in-law, James McKee and family. Henry remembers that he, too, worked for Melvin during haying and harvest for the going wage then of fifty cents a day. Melvin often told the boys about articles stored on the second story floor of the barn, relics of Ashbel's early farm operations—a cradle for harvesting grain, a flail for separating the grain from the chaff, wooden forks and shovels, ox yokes, a box of oxen shoes in assorted sizes, since a shoe was fitted to each toe of an oxen's cloven hoof.

A Farm and Barn By the Side of a Road

Melvin told the boys of the days when 16 horses were stabled there and cattle were fed for market; about his father Ashbel buying the original acreage from the United States government for $1.25 an acre and plowing with oxen a trench around it to mark its boundary, since fences were hard to come by in those early days. He told about using the cradle and flail to harvest and thresh those first crops of wheat and barley, of hauling the wheat to Chicago with an ox team—a slow, three-week round trip, and how pleased he was to have enough left to buy a new shirt after the wheat was exchanged for a few bare necessities.

As Henry recalls, there was a lean-to at the west end of the barn that was used as a cow barn. By 1920, not many horses were left, but Ring and Daze were kept, a fat, faithful team well known in the neighborhood. Melvin liked good horses and had trained them to pull tight on the bit, but if anyone else drove, they relaxed. Ring, a bay, had circles of white hair around the upper part of his tail and Daze (for Daisy) was a white horse. In 1915, Melvin bought his first automobile, a 4-cylinder Reo which he traded the following year for a 6-cylinder, 7-passenger car. One always knew when Melvin was going to town, because the car would roar in low gear until he got safely down the hill to the west of the schoolhouse.

The Crouch School

The Crouch families, Ashbel, Melvin and Dwight, were honest, thrifty, and believed in education to the point of giving an acre of ground just north of the house to be used for educational purposes for $4.00 a year, later raised to $6.00, for the site of the Crouch School, the fourth of the eight one-room schools to be built in Ustick. When the one-room schools were closed by the state, the land reverted to the farm, but the school house itself belonged to the district. When the Meremas bought the farm that acre was included, and to avoid moving the schoolhouse they bought it for $300.00 and converted it to a corncrib.

The first school election was held April 4, 1856, in the home of Ashbel Crouch, called by the treasurer of the township board of school trustees. Clark Abbott, John A. Crouch and Ashbel Crouch were elected directors and the first school building soon was started.

A Farm and Barn By the Side of a Road

Years later, that building is said to have been moved to the Levi Lewis farm and a bigger, better building erected.

The former Crouch School, where Mrs. Abbott taught before her marriage in 1923, now serves as a corn crib, on the original site at the corner of Union Grove and Millard Roads in Ustick Township.

One of the first teachers, Lucy Crawford, received $48.00 for the summer term of 12 weeks. An entry of 1863 says, "As there has been a tax levied of 75 cents on the $100.00 taxable property in the district, the income for this year will be about $200.00. That will leave the directors the sum of $142.00 to carry on our school for the next year, which will be the sum of $22.00 more than last year and pay off all indebtedness. We would recommend to the new board of directors to hire a competent male teacher for this winter, as the necessities of the district demand such a one."

By the time the last school house was built, Buikema recalls, a big Cottonwood tree had grown in the yard where the building was to be placed. Rather than go to the extra work and expense of grubbing out the roots, the directors decided to just build the school house over the stump. When some years later the state decreed a different heating system, a narrow passage had to be dug along the east wall to give access to a furnace room in the basement. Henry remembers his father telling about sawing down the huge tree with a cross cut saw—no chain saws in those days! Dwight Crouch served as a director of the school in the 1930s, the school he had attended for eight years.

Since the first parcel of land was bought in 1854, three homes have been built on it, two still are occupied. The first, like the barn, was built big, but, like the barn, became obsolete and expensive to maintain. Dwight had never married but lived in the house until his death.

A second, two-story, square house for a tenant family was built in the same yard by contractor Arie Post, of Fulton, for $3,100.00. Following Dwight's death in 1950, the original big house was torn down. The Jacob J. Dykstra family rented the farm at one time and lived in the square house. Mrs. Dykstra and son Clarence, now living in Fulton, recall many things about the farm and especially the big barn, although many changes had been made over the years. Horse power had given way to tractor power. The horse barn on the east end was used for 14 milk cows, and another 16 to 18 were accommodated in the west end. Calving stalls also were used. A water system had been installed for individual cups to the milk cows, and there were two oat bins in each cattle barn. Plank floors had worn out and been replaced with concrete.

A third house was built north of the square house by George Balk during his brief ownership. The very modern, one-story ranch type home is enjoyed now by the Merema family.

Memories of a Schoolteacher

We learned to know the Melvin Crouch family well during the months we taught at the Crouch School and were privileged to live in the home. Mrs. Margaret McKee Crouch was a kind, motherly woman to everyone, and to some children in the district she always was Aunt Maggie. Melvin Crouch, a staunch Democrat, had very definite ideas about honesty in business dealings, often saying a man's word should be as good as his bond. Dwight, their son, was a pupil in the school who tried hard to do things right, and a good student. As a family they were kind and considerate of one another.

A Farm and Barn By the Side of a Road

Their home was one of the first in the area to have a central heating system, indoor plumbing, and a carbide plant for lighting the home. Mrs. Crouch loved her home and the furnishings that had been handed down from her husband's parents. It was a joy to come home from school, open the door and smell the fresh bread, pies and cakes she could turn out. Good New England breakfasts of pancakes and sausage could start a perfect day.

All enjoyed reading and had a variety of magazines, the local weekly newspapers and the Chicago Daily Drovers Journal handy to read at night after the supper dishes were cleared from the dining table. Neighbors who did not subscribe to papers would send someone to ask for old newspapers when "Ma is going to clean the cupboards and the pantry and needs some for the shelves."

A family joke concerned slow, early rural mail delivery. Melvin went by rail from Fulton to Nebraska on a business trip, leaving instructions for the family to meet him at the depot in Fulton on his return, at a time he would indicate by letter when his errand was completed. Ample time was allowed for the letter to reach home, but when he arrived early that morning no one was there to meet him. So without wasting any time he picked up his suitcase and walked the six miles, stopped at the mailbox at his driveway, got out the mail that had been delivered that morning and carried his letter into the house himself.

Teacher's wages in those days--$57.50 per calendar month, no holidays except Thanksgiving, Christmas and New Year's, but in three years they zoomed to $90.00 a month due to inflation at the time of World War I. A teacher taught all eight grades, did all the janitor work, attended five days of Institute in August and two in February on her own time—and was glad to have a job. Broken contracts and strikes would have been unthinkable.

Some schools required classes to be held between Christmas and New Year's, particularly if those two legal holidays occurred on weekends. Any day except legal holidays were "made up" on later weekends in the spring or at the end of the school year.

The Ashbel Crouch family, Melvin's parents, were lovers, too, of law and order. Since federal laws had been enacted making the giving of help or comfort to a runaway slave an offense punishable by fine and/or imprisonment, they were not sympathetic toward the

A Farm and Barn By the Side of a Road

Underground Railroad that developed in the Cottonwood area toward Blind Charley's Corner, and beyond toward Canada and freedom for runaways. Care was taken in passing the frightened black slaves to the next "station" that they were well concealed as they passed the Crouch farm.

*The Crouch School bell was relocated to the Merema's yard,
just south of the school site.*

Modern Times

The present owners, Mr. and Mrs. Robert Merema, who acquired the 200-acre home place of the Crouch holding in 1958 and moved there the following year have made many changes. The big barn is the last of the original buildings to go, so only the rather modern former "wash house" remains. It houses the water system that supplies water to the two homes and the livestock operations. Six or seven dug wells were found in the yard and fields near the buildings. Abandoned as water sources, the walls had caved in but left holes hazardous to machinery operations and livestock, and were filled in.

Three Harvestore silos have replaced barns, one 25' x 80', two 20' x 60'; one holds haylage, one corn and one high-moisture shelled corn. No hogs, chickens or horses are raised. All cattle feeding is done by push button, and automatic waterers supply the tanks.

Family help furnishes manpower in peak seasons. A son-in-law, Lester Dierks of Preston, Iowa, helps in haying season to chop for the big silos. A son, Kenneth Merema, of Fulton, who is a truck driver for Air Co., of Clinton, plans time to help combine the corn. Father, Clarence Merema, of Fulton, can be called on to help when needed. Other family members are Mrs. Lester Dierks, of Preston; Roberta, at home; and Stanley, who is a purchasing manager for DeKalb Agriculture Co., at DeKalb, Ill. The square tenant house is rented to Mr. and Mrs. Kenneth Wiersema, who are employed elsewhere.

One might think Bob and Theresa would find the work on the farm more than enough, but not so. Bob enjoys driving a big truck, hauls grain for Harold Smith's corn sheller and feed for the Farmer's Elevator of Morrison. Theresa enjoys her lovely lawn, where the big bell from the Crouch School is installed. She "just likes to mow grass," so with her riding mower keeps even the old schoolyard as neat as her own.

Pioneer Legacy Lives On

Marble monuments mark the graves in the Cottonwood Community Cemetery of the members of the Crouch family, pioneers in agriculture in the township of Ustick. Their big barn, so long a landmark, is gone, too. It was taken down by a man from rural Savanna, the heavy timbers saved to reuse, the wide siding boards saved to be used by builders of new homes to give their family rooms and rec rooms that popular "weathered antique look."

Most interesting is the use that may be made of hundreds of old square nails that Theresa has picked up and saved to be offered to Stanley Maxfield, a member of the Morrison United Methodist Church. When the church was remodeled and enlarged several years ago, many square nails were saved from the old parts of the building. Pastor Bruce Brenneman suggested to Mr. Maxfield that a suitable memento be made from the nails to present to each member of the confirmation class of young folks when they became members of the church. Two of the nails, cleaned of rust and coated with a clear protective substance are held in the shape of a cross by a brass ring

A Farm and Barn By the Side of a Road

soldered to hold them in place, and the assembly suspended on a narrow leather thong to be worn around the neck if desired.

Mr. Maxfield has enjoyed the unusual hobby and has made and presented to graduates of the confirmation classes more than 100 of the crosses to serve as reminders of the crucifixion and also as reminders of the debt present generations owe to the organizers and builders of the first church, from which the nails came.

Harold Sikkema of Fulton has acquired some heavy timbers from the old Crouch barn to use in a hobby he has been pursuing since 1967. Well-seasoned white pine and basswood are his favorite materials, and good, knot-free old wood makes fine duck decoys.

Since retiring a few years ago, Sikkema keeps busy in his basement workshop where he spends as much as two weeks turning out a realistic ornamental decoy. They are replicas of birds indigenous to this flyway area—wood ducks, blue wing and green wing teals, mallards, canvas backs, red heads, green bills, pin tails, even a pair of spoon bills to fill an order. He knows first-hand the shapes, colors and characteristics of the ducks from many years of hunting in duck blinds along the Mississippi.

If remnants of the old Crouch barn can be made into crosses, mantelpieces, rec room paneling, and carved ducks, what will these shiny blue Harvestore silos, that are replacing the barns, be recycled into a hundred years from now, when they become worn out and obsolete?

27. A Tale of Nine Lives—Minus Two

April 1978

Thomas Catt, chief mouse catcher for the James Aggen family at their dairy farm at Union Grove, returned recently from an unscheduled weekend with friends and enemies in Moline.

The big, sleek, black cat adjusted his full tummy to the soft, clean straw near the cat pan in the barn, stretched appreciatively, flexed his paws and recounted some of his adventures, somewhat as follows, for the welcoming committee of cats and kittens nearby:

"There's no place like home. As you know, we seldom get much farther from home than Bull's Elevator where sometimes we help cut down the mouse population in a busy season. But don't ever let anybody lure you away with talk of the big city. I've been there—it's no place for country cats.

"Another thing I must warn you about is the danger of climbing up the warm differential of a truck or car on cool mornings. It was a cold Friday recently when I was kidnapped as I catnapped on the warm differential of the big milk truck making the last stop of the day to pick up milk produced by our boss, James Aggen. It was nice and warm up there under the truck and I must have dozed off.

"Suddenly, the truck was moving and I hung onto that dishpan sized differential for dear life as it moved down the road. Such a wind, and cold, too, and such jolts—all the way to Baker Dairy in Moline. I'm certain one of my nine lives was expended on that ride as I tried to dig my claws into the metal to keep from falling under the wheels.

"When the truck—and the jolting—stopped I admit I cried a bit, maybe even yowled with relief, only to bring new troubles to myself. Men came looking for "that cat," but I hung on to the underside of the truck, afraid to get off among strangers. Finally they dragged in a hose and turned a stream of cold water on me that washed me right to the floor—only to be set upon by a big, fierce barking dog!

"Luckily, a tree was just outside. Soaked to the skin and shivering with fright, I scrambled up the tree out of reach of the dog and here I spent a miserable night huddled against a limb. With the shower, the dog, and the cold night in the tree I lost at least another of my nine lives—leaving me seven.

"The wind was so cold, I'd had no supper, so I didn't sleep much but I did learn a few tricks that city dogs and cats use to survive. From my perch in the tree I observed that after the lights go out in most of the houses, hungry dogs prowl the garbage cans and bags for a bit of food. I'd no more than be catching a wink of sleep when another garbage can lid would be clanging. When the dogs moved on, the hungry cats picked over the trash again, but I was afraid to join them.

"Morning came at last, but all that long day I spent trying to stay out of sight of dogs and strange people, and getting hungrier all the time. The next day was the same, but I did recognize our regular milk hauler and I think, after I dried out from the hosing, that he began to remember me, for we had always been good friends at home. I heard him telling another man he had asked our boss when he was back on the route on Monday if he were short one big black cat, and our boss said I hadn't been seen at the cat pan for several days. Things began to look brighter for me after that.

"Early Tuesday morning, our regular hauler offered me a carton of delicious cottage cheese if I would jump up into the cab of the milk truck with him. The cheese smelled so good and I was SO hungry I couldn't resist (although I now distrust trucks, at least the undersides of them).

"The cab was warm, the seat soft, the cheese so good, and the hauler so kind, I decided to take a chance on getting home, so I agreed to go along. Between stops to pick up milk, the hauler let me sleep on his lap so by the time we made the last stop of the day to pick up Aggen's milk, I was in pretty good shape and oh-so-glad to be home and to find a warm supper waiting for me in our own cat pan!

"I'm still tired from the hijacking and I need some sleep, so you kittens tend to the mouse chores while I enjoy this late afternoon sunshiny spot and nap a while. Having at best only seven lives left, I must conserve my health and energy, you know. You might go up to the house yard and look around. Our lady boss, like most ladies, has a sort of a hangup about mice and appreciates seeing you on patrol. Mind your manners and she may have a few table scraps saved for you.

"And don't you cats and kittens ever forget—there's no place like home, but if you're ever stranded in Moline, Jack Baker and Herb Noah are good men to know. Run along now and maybe I'll tell you more stories later."

28. Old Settlers' Log Cabins Dedicated at 1885 Fair

July 1981

With the 111th annual Whiteside County Fair only a month away, it might be well to remember the good old days when the only vacation a farm family took was a day or two at the Fair each year. Thanks to the courtesy of Mr. and Mrs. Wayne Entwhistle of Morrison, who share a page from their scrapbook of pictures and clippings kept by his mother, the late Mrs. Arthur J. Entwhistle, we can include an item that may interest the descendants of folks that attended the Fair the first week of September 1885.

Early in August of that year, anyone who had settled in this county on or before 1840 was invited by the officers of the Fair (called then the Whiteside County Central Agricultural Society) to furnish a log 16 feet in length and 12- to 14-inches in diameter, to be used to build a log cabin as a memorial to the old settlers of the county, and to come on Aug. 20 to help build the cabin.

So many logs were donated that the 86 old settlers who came to build the cabin decided to build not one but three—a single and a double cabin, and have them finished and furnished by Sept. 1. In the east cabin, the sill and window in the east wall were from the first cabin built in Garden Plain township by Abel Parker in 1836.

Pioneer Ingenuity Guided Amateur Carpenters

Remembering that the logs were to be brought to the building site in the rough, some perhaps long or short of the specified 16 feet, and of varying diameters and curves, what a Tower of Babel must have developed as some 86 amateur pioneer carpenters sorted and assigned the material as it arrived that first day.

Old Settlers' Log Cabins Dedicated at 1885 Fair

The make-it-do ingenuity of the pioneers solved the problems as they arose and by the end of a week the logs for the three cabins were notched and fitted in place. Windows and entrances, rough but sturdy and adequate, were installed and the roof made tight against the weather, even with the addition of a chimney.

Songs, Speeches Highlight Old Settlers' Program

In the good old days, it was a long drive with a 16-foot log, or logs, in a lumber wagon from the far corners of the county to Morrison to help build the memorial cabins at the fairgrounds. But by 1885, the Chicago and Northwestern railroad had crossed the state, and getting to the Fair by train from points along its route was an adventure in itself.

Most folks, though, still came with horse-drawn vehicles. Chores were done early that morning, the big picnic dinner with fried chicken, homemade rolls, fresh apple pies, cake, pickles, jams and other goodies was loaded into the wagon. Then the family, all in freshly starched Sunday best climbed in and they were off before the sun could make the day hot and dusty.

More than 400 old settlers who had lived in the county on or before 1840 were on hand Sept. 2, 1885 for the dedication of the memorial cabins, were admitted free of charge at the gate, and had their pictures taken. The program lasted all day, with a break at noon for the picnic dinner.

The president, Col. E. Seely, called the fairgoers to order at 11:30 a.m. and prayer was offered by Rev. A.M. Early of Erie. The Old Settlers' Choir sang "America" with cornet accompaniment. The dedicatory address was given by Prof. M.R. Kelly, and the band played. After the noon meal, the Old Settlers' Choir sang "Auld Lang Syne," led by cornet. Five-minute speeches were given by old settlers, the choir and the audience sang "Old Hundred," and the program ended with "informal visiting and hand-shaking."

Certainly a full day. Probably the sun was getting low, Father brought the horses that had been tied to a tree, hitched them up, loaded the family and went home to do chores and think about what a wonderful day it had been.

Old Settlers' Log Cabins Dedicated at 1885 Fair

Old Settlers First Clustered Near Rivers
August 1981

In the good old days, the availability of wood and water often determined the location a settler's family chose for the site of its cabin home. Wood for building and for fuel had to be cut, and water had to be carried from a spring or stream, which accounts for the fact that the townships along the Rock River and Mississippi River, and those traversed by the early stage routes, attracted the most settlers before the 1840s. Thus, those townships responded with more logs to build the memorial cabins than could the others farther inland.

The records show that seven old settlers from Albany promised logs; 15 from Lyndon intended to be on hand with logs and help. A Genesee settler wrote that five persons from that town would furnish logs, the only persons then living in the township who had settled there prior to 1840. Ten old settlers from Mt. Pleasant township agreed to bring logs and help with the county-wide project. As word of the proposed memorial got around, more persons found they could qualify as donors, and many brought more than one log.

Fifteen kinds of wood were used in the cabins. Donors were urged to furnish logs that would be most durable and included black walnut, white ash, blue ash, red elm, white oak, burr oak, red oak, black oak, chestnut, cottonwood, pine, cherry, hackberry, poplar and butternut. The donor's name was painted on the logs he contributed.

Logs for the entryway were given as follows: P.B. Pollock, Hopkins township, 1835; John Kent, Mt. Pleasant, 1839; E.J. Ewers, Fenton, 1839; C.H. Slocumb, Albany, 1839; and A. Zoirns, Garden Plain, 1845. Lists for the east, west and south cabins as they were designated, follow, including the donor's name, township and year the family settled in Whiteside County.

East Cabin Log Donors

Name of the donor	Township	Year
L.S. Pennington	Jordan	1839
Warren, Ezekial and Walker Olds	Albany	1838
Col. E. Seely	Portland	1834
Wm. B. Paschal	Mt. Pleasant	1835

Old Settlers' Log Cabins Dedicated at 1885 Fair

Name of the donor	Township	Year
A.J. Seely	Portland	1836
S.M. Seely	Portland	1836
W.H. Colcord	Genesee	1839
Mrs. Nancy Paschal	Mt. Pleasant	1835
R.T. Hughes	Mt. Pleasant	1839
O. Baker	Mt. Pleasant	1839
S.M. Coe	Jordan	1835
A. Farrington	Mt. Pleasant	1836
Chas. McMullen	Mt. Pleasant	1838
Frank Parker	Garden Plain	1836
Calvin Williams	Prophetstown	1837
E. Parker	Garden Plain	1836
C.F. Adams	Portland	1839
O.T. Clark	Prophetstown	1836
Mrs. M.J. Knox	Mt. Pleasant	1839
D.O. Coe	Jordan	1838
G.R. Hamilton	Lyndon	1835
M.V. Seely	Prophetstown	1836
Judge James McCoy	Fulton	1837
H.H. Holbrook	Genesee	1838
Truman Parker	Garden Plain	1836
Mrs. R. Parker	Garden Plain	1836
Mrs. A.P. Young	Mt. Pleasant	1835
A.A. James	Mt. Pleasant	1837
T.B. Eaton	Garden Plain	1836
Mrs. M. Sweet	Garden Plain	1836
Mrs. S.T. Grinnold	Garden Plain	1839
Mrs. A.L. Hazard	Lyndon	1837
F.J. Jackson	Mt. Pleasant	1838
M.G. Wood	Genesee	1836
C.R. Rood	Garden Plain	1836
E.B. Warner	Mt. Pleasant	1838
Henry Rexroat	Newton	1836
Mrs. Phoebe Vennum	Union Grove	Unk.
J.C. Young	Union Grove	1837
T.W. Stevens	Sterling	1836

Old Settlers' Log Cabins Dedicated at 1885 Fair

South Cabin Log Donors

Name of the donor	Township	Year
H. Brinks	Sterling	1834
P.B. Besse	Portland	1835
John J. Knox	Mt. Pleasant	1835
J.N. Hamilton	Lyndon	1835
Mrs. Peter Knox	Mt. Pleasant	1835
Mrs. B.F. Lathe	Lyndon	1835
Henry L. Knox	Mt. Pleasant	1835
Mrs. A. Knox	Mt. Pleasant	1835
J.D. Fenton	Erie	1835
E.B. Hill	Prophetstown	1835
C.F. Lusk	Albany	1836
J.M. Eaton	Garden Plain	1836
Rachel Hardy	Sterling	1836
Capt. S.B. Hanks	Albany	1836
Mrs. E. Vannum	Union Grove	1837
H.D. Burch	Union Grove	1837
W.Y. Ives	Fulton	1837
Mrs. M. Town	Clyde	1837
H.C. Meeys	Fulton	1837
Mrs. M. George	unknown	1835
E. H. Nevitt	Albany	1837
John Coburn	Mt. Pleasant	1837
J.W. Hazard	Lyndon	1837
John Abbey	Newton	1837
Solomon Hubbard	Lyndon	1838
Robert C. Andrews	Sterling	1838
Mrs. L.B. Crosby	Mt. Pleasant	1838
Oliver Hall	Mt. Pleasant	1838
M.P. Warner	Mt. Pleasant	1838

Old Settlers' Log Cabins Dedicated at 1885 Fair

Name of the donor	Township	Year
J.Y. Jackson	Union Grove	1838
Mrs. W.H. Judd	Mt. Pleasant	1838
Henry Baum	Mt. Pleasant	1838
E.C. Hutchinson	Prophetstown	1839
John Scott	Hopkins	1939
C.P. Emory	Mt. Pleasant	1839
J.D. O'Dell	Mt. Pleasant	1839
Capt. W.S. Barnes	Albany	1839
W.S. Wilkinson	Mt. Pleasant	1839
A.T. Thompson	Newton	1839
Mrs. H.C. Donaldson	Mt. Pleasant	1839
Mrs. Julia T. Russell	Sterling	1839
Mrs. Florence H. Whitman	Hopkins	1839
Albert S. Sampson	Sterling	1839
S. Currie	Mt. Pleasant	1839
J.M. Dodd	Mt. Pleasant	1839
A.J. Tuller	Prophetstown	1840
Sullivan Jackson	Mt. Pleasant	1840

West Cabin Log Donors

George O. James	Mt. Pleasant	1835
L.C. Reynolds	Prophetstown	1835
W.F. Boyer	Mt. Pleasant	1835
W.D. Dudley	Lyndon	1835
G.W. Thomas	Mt. Pleasant	1835
A.W. Fenton	Erie	1835
Capt. J.M. Burr	Hopkins	1835
Art Thompson	Portland	1836
Richard Thompson	Portland	1836
R.J. Thompson	Portland	1836
J.S. Logan	Prophetstown	1836

Old Settlers' Log Cabins Dedicated at 1885 Fair

Name of the donor	Township	Year
Mrs. H.M. Grinnold	Fulton	1836
Wm. H. Thompson	Portland	1836
E.S. Gage	Prophetstown	1836
T. Dudley	Prophetstown	1836
H. Parker	Garden Plain	1836
J.R. Thompson	Portland	1836
J.P. Fuller	Portland	1836
John C. Swarthout	Lyndon	1836
G.W. Brewer	Sterling	1836
Enos Williams	Portland	1837
F.N. Brewer	Lyndon	1837
B.P. Brewer	Lyndon	1837
Mrs. Robert C. McClendenin	Mt. Pleasant	1837
P.A. Brooks	Lyndon	1837
D.B. Young	Mt. Pleasant	1837
Mrs. P.B. Vannest	Garden Plain	1837
A.I. Maxwell	Lyndon	1837
W.C. Thomas	Mt. Pleasant	1837
Rodney Crook	Prophetstown	1838
J.A. Sweet	Garden Plain	1839
A. Adams	Portland	1839
L. Culbertson	Garden Plain	1839
J.W. Gage	Prophetstown	1839
Z. Demp	Clyde	1839
L.B. Ramsey	Prophetstown	1839
Donald Blue	Clyde	1839
Mrs. B.J. Ackerman	Clyde	1839
Daniel Blue	Clyde	1839
M.A. Green	Ustick	1840
Mrs. F. Hopkins Angell	Hopkins	1840

29. Log Cabins Stood for Half Century

August 1981

The log cabins at the Whiteside County Fairgrounds were enjoyed by fairgoers for more than half a century when they stood north of the amphitheater near the race track, where concession stands, food and games of chance are now offered. Most of the pioneers who had provided the logs and labor to build and furnish the three cabins had died and, lacking a continuing and interested source of upkeep, the cabins fell into disrepair. They became victims of the weather, and as now, of vandals. Officers of the Fair Association changed with the years.

With the beginning of the Great Depression about 1930, Fair attendance fell off as folks lacked money for much beyond bare necessities. There was no money to repair buildings, particularly unused structures like the cabins on the grounds. During those "desperate years," so little was realized from gate receipts that concessionaires could not pay their fees and there was not enough income to pay the premiums that had been offered for exhibits.

Since the holders of season tickets are actually the voting policy group, they were asked to contribute an extra ten dollars each (or more, if they really believed in county fairs) to pay the premiums which were an obligation made by the Fair board, the elected officials chosen by the season ticket holders—just as bank stockholders at that time were liable for the deposits in a bank and were so assessed. Most of the season ticket holders responded, and the credit of the association remained sound. But there was no surplus for repairs or replacements during those hard years. By 1939, the cabins had reached a state of musty deterioration and were torn down.

30. Fair Week was Vacation Time

August 1982

One of the year's busiest weeks in many households around Morrison will be Aug. 17-21, dates of the Whiteside County Fair.

Exhibitors are studying the premium lists for the many departments that will be giving away more than $88,000 in premiums this year.

Seed catalogs that promised bountiful yields last spring were studied for the right variety to plant in time for exhibit this month. Now comes the moment of truth when entries are judged and ribbons awarded.

Many new classes will be offered. The Junior divisions present chances for the young folks to earn premiums. The new metal exhibit buildings will be filled with the results of hours and hours of work—vegetables, fruits, flowers, baking and food preservation, sewing and crafts of so many kinds. The Hobby department has a category for nearly everyone to enter. Chances to excel with entries are many in livestock.

In the good old days, fair-going was for many farm families the only vacation they had and some arranged to spend every day there—seeing the machinery, livestock, visiting friends they might not see again until the next fair, riding the merry-go-round at five cents a trip, or thrilling at a ride down the shoot-the-chutes, maybe risking a nickel on a bingo game or a toss at the lucky game to win a pretty dish as a souvenir to take home.

Always there was a big picnic dinner at noon, spread under a shade tree, the white linen tablecloth surrounded by blankets and cushions for seats, then a stick of taffy to chew on the way home.

Fair Week was Vacation Time

At day's end, everyone tired, clothes dirty, Mother always managed to have things ready for a fresh, clean start to the Fair next morning as soon as chores were done.

Lucky Kids Went Every Day

A critic offers feedback on the statement last week that children, fresh and clean, attended the Fair every day.

Not so, he says. At his house, one day was all one could be sure of, because every spring at school election, contracts were let for fall cleaning of the yard and schoolhouse in preparation for the opening of school.

His father often bid for the yard cleaning and his mother on the schoolhouse job, each of which went to the lowest bid that might be around $15 for each. Thirty dollars was a lot of money in those days, enough for the family's school books and maybe a new dinner pail or pencil box.

School never started until after the Morrison Fair, which usually was the last few days of August and the first day or so of September. And school started on Monday. Labor Day was just another Monday as far as rural thinking went, but school couldn't begin before the Fair.

To mow, rake and tidy up the school yard just the week before school started kept father and the boys busy, while mother and the girls swept, scrubbed and dusted the building. All this activity interfered with daily attendance at the Fair. Maybe some lucky kids went every day, but this lad spent most of the week raking the school yard.

Boys Deliver Pumpkins, Cookies for Judging

People remember funny things as years change perspective. The boy inspired by the pumpkins one year decided that next year he would raise and enter some at the Fair. Seeds he planted turned out to be pie pumpkins instead of huge cow pumpkins. But they grew fast, and were ripe in time, and he made his entry.

Came the day to take them for exhibit, his father needed the car for his job, so the boy brought the required three pumpkins, all at one time, on his bicycle! Ever try to ride a bike and carry three pumpkins? He couldn't do it now.

Fair Week was Vacation Time

Or consider the boy whose first try for premium at the fair was in the Junior culinary department, a department in those days with only a very few classes.

He remembers sitting on the kitchen floor with a mixing bowl between his legs, stirring and stirring the ingredients he had carefully measured out for a batch of drop cookies. Another basket of cobs for the old cookstove, and the oven was just right. The best dozen cookies, placed on a paper plate, were entered.

Then came the suspense of waiting until they were judged. Arriving for the day, he raced to the old Floral Hall to see, and sure enough, there was a blue ribbon on his plate of cookies. This being before the day of a pay phone on the grounds, he asked the Fair secretary if he could call home to tell his mother, and was allowed to do so.

Beautiful Trees Shaded Weary Visitors

One of the things many folks miss at the Fair now are the beautiful shade trees that made it one of the coolest, most comfortable fairgrounds in this part of the state.

Heavy plank seating surrounded many of the trees, so weary fairgoers could drop down to rest on the sunny or shady side, as weather indicated. Each of these permanent circular seats could accommodate from six to a dozen folks.

The Dutch elm disease and oak blight killed most of the trees. Young trees have been planted to replace them, but a good tree grows slowly and must be protected from accident and vandalism.

Work Came Before the Fair

We got some additions to the recent account of the not-so-good old days during the recession of the early 1930s. The woman who remembers the hundreds of quarts of fruit and vegetables her mother canned every year to fill the shelves in the fruit cellar. Another friend says she raised and canned at least 100 quarts of tomatoes, and a like amount of tomato juice each year, in addition to similar quantities of homegrown fruits and other vegetables—all canned with the heat from the big old kitchen stove. No electricity and, of course, no electric fan or air conditioning.

Fair Week was Vacation Time

Another home industry popular then was making up batches of soap from the surplus lard from home butchering, before the day of the locker. Lard and other fats were combined with lye, some of the lye even homemade from the wood ashes from the old cook stove—nothing went to waste!

The ideal homemade soap was a white mass about the consistency of cake batter, poured into a box or pan to a depth of about an inch or more, allowed to cool and harden, then cut into cakes in squares or oblongs and stored for future use. A cake of such soap sliced thin and allowed to soften overnight in the wash boiler for next day's laundry turned out beautifully white clothes. Until just a few years ago, premiums were offered at the Morrison Fair each year for best entries of a plate of homemade soap.

Fair Echoes
August 1983

A former resident of the Morrison/Fulton area who read the stories of the good old days at the Morrison Fair has contributions of their own.

This one from central Illinois covers several generations of fairgoers: "As you know, the Fair was right up there with Christmas, the Fourth of July, even Thanksgiving. I'm sure I thought it was a national holiday. Benevolent school districts always gave Thursday off and many were the tears if it should rain on that day. Lucky parents could go Friday and Saturday, but the latter was a poor substitute for a youngster. It was only a half a day and the exhibits, rides, etc. were being taken down.

"My father, born in 1854, insisted he'd gone to the first fair, and according to history it's entirely possible. In 1856, he would have had his second birthday on Aug. 30. I even have a tiny red calico coat his mother made for him to wear. The color was a wise choice because in spite of all diligence, he became lost. He finally was discovered on the ground directly under the platform where the parlor pump organ was standing. Always fond of music, he'd gotten himself a ringside seat for the agricultural program. A nearby gentleman volunteered that he'd tried to help Dad catch a straying rooster just prior.

Fair Week was Vacation Time

"My parents never found much in my early conversation worthy of an anecdote, but there is one exception. Time passed, and it was in 1902 or 1903 and they had a toddler ready to sample the Fair. I ran through the several changes of clean clothing my mother had taken along, I'd bumped my head and screamed lustily, I'd enjoyed a pacifying gift (from a bystander) of very sticky candy—all the routine things, and my babysitters were ready to call it an 'early' day.

"As I was being led away, I was said to have joyfully remarked: 'Baby did have a good time at the Morrison Fair.' Legend also has it that my remark was capped by my father's mutter: 'I'm glad someone did.'"

Harness racing drew big crowds to the amphitheatre and shady infield at the Whiteside County Fair in Morrison in the early 1960s.

31. Fair Reflects Our Changing Society

August 1982

Many things have changed for the better in 112 years since the Whiteside County Agricultural Association started with nothing more than a vision, and the founders couldn't have imagined the present week's activities.

Fortunately, it still adheres to the dream it had of showing the beauty and importance of the area's farming potential and accomplishments, plus relaxation and fun for everyone who chooses to cooperate in such a democratic organization.

Many years ago, one father lined up the four children before leaving for a day at the fair. Starting with the oldest boy, about 10, he asked him how much money he would need that day to spend. After careful thought, the lad asked for a quarter. Next in line was the small daughter who thought she could get along on 10 cents. The next, a boy, said he could do with a nickel but really would like a dime, too; then he could get both a bottle of strawberry pop and a ride on the merry-go-round. Turning to the small boy at the end of the line, the father said: "Well, son, how much will you need today?" Quick as a flash came the answer: "I want a dollar," an amount unheard of—it was a day's wages at hard work for a man. How times have changed!

Music, Dust and a Day of Emancipation

In the good old days, folks walked to the Fairgrounds if they lived in Morrison. Country folks came in horse-drawn vehicles. The Chicago and Northwestern Railroad ran a special train from Fulton to Morrison in the morning and returned in the evening. A horse-drawn hack, seating about a dozen, made the trips from the depot to the Fairgrounds.

Libby's Band, a sort of loose organization of excellent musicians who played because they loved to, formed uptown on Main Street and played its way to the Fair about mid-morning, sending into tantrums any country horses who also happened to be on the route, who had never heard so much noise and all but ran away when the slide trombone was aimed their way.

In dry weather, the roads through the grounds were deep with dust that swirled in clouds—but then, so were all roads in those days. A great improvement was the periodic trips, made several times a day, of the big sprinkling wagon to wet down the dust and reduce it to mud. Now, all-weather roads cut down the dust and mud problems.

Clothes, too, are different. Going to the Fair in the good old days was one of the year's dress-up social events. Couples arriving on the special train sometimes had matching color suits or coats. Ladies wore beautiful big Merry Widow hats with plumes or flowers, feather boas and ankle-length skirts, of course. The founding fathers would be amazed at the informality of dress now evident at fairs.

Refreshments then and now: A complete meal, with homemade pie and plenty of coffee cost 35 cents; ice cream cones (double dip) a nickel; popcorn, five cents a bag, caramel corn hadn't been invented yet that wasn't too sticky. Fortunately there was no beer garden and liquor never was sold in the grounds. Pizza hadn't gotten this far West yet; no foot-long hot dogs or milk shakes either.

One woman of our acquaintance took the only vacation she had attending the Fair every day if possible. She so enjoyed sitting on a chair or stool at a food tent, having a meal without one bit of preparation on her part, placed before her, eating it leisurely, and walking away without having to wash a single dish or pan. She was emancipated for a day! The remainder of the day she spent playing Bingo, accumulating such little prizes that might come her way, and visiting with friends.

"Norma, The Wild Girl Captured in the Highest Mountains of Tibet, Hear Her Growl"

Some types of entertainment, too, have disappeared from the grounds. No more monstrosities or freaks of nature are shown. The farmer who maybe had a three-legged colt, a two-headed sheep or five-legged calf or some other abnormal animal born on his farm sought to turn unprofitable livestock into moneymakers by setting up a tent and charging admission to view his misfortune—obviously not in line with the original fair dream of showing as near-perfect entries as possible.

Boxing and wrestling exhibitions and matches that often involved local competitors also are no more. Sideshows that come along with the midway carnival also are carefully screened. For instance—a young man, seeking his fortune, went out West hoping to find work in the harvest fields as the season worked North, but found the crews already made up and not hiring any unskilled help. He soon ran out of money and applied for a roustabout job with a carnival that was set up that week in a town in Kansas.

The owner told him the only job open was because Norma had quit the day before. If he could take her place he could join the carnival. Food would be simple but ample, he could sleep in one of the tents, there wouldn't be much pay, but since they were heading East playing as many towns as would admit them, he could work his way home.

Billed as "Norma, The Wild Girl Captured in the Highest Mountains of Tibet, Hear Her Growl," she made very brief stage appearances outside the tent to draw the crowd in, which then viewed her from a platform around a four-foot deep pit. Clad in a mangy old fur cape, a hula-type grass skirt, long clay fingernails and a stringy black hair wig, Norma uttered shrieks of pain and anguish as she tried to scale the sides of her pit pen that had only a bit of straw and a pan of water for furniture.

So realistic was her performance, the good ladies of the churches in some of the towns sought to "rescue that pitiful creature." So, if Norma comes to Illinois look her over carefully. She may be your next-door neighbor working his way home—"pay forfeited if you quit before your contract is completed." But she won't be at Morrison.

State Line Rides, that has supplied the midway at Morrison for years, ran a pretty tight ship on the company. Anyone getting out of line very far would be out of a job and set adrift. It was sold recently to Mike Armstrong, of Louisiana, who furnishes the rides and carnival-type entertainment this year.

Fair Reflects Our Changing Society

Vanished with the One-Room School

One of the good things that flourished and vanished with the one-room school was the School Department, which was housed in the northwest corner of the big Floral Hall on the hill. During a school year, a teacher and her pupils would prepare samples of writing, drawing, free-hand silhouette work and other crafts. These would be entered for premiums earned for the individuals or for the school to buy some desired books, maps, or perhaps a picture for the wall that the district budget did not include.

The county Superintendent of Schools and one assistant office helper comprised the office force at the court house, so teachers set up the fair display. Two kindly ladies, who arranged their homemade fancywork for display and sale in a three-cornered booth on a raised platform in a corner of the hall, kept a watchful eye on the school exhibit. Vandalism was unheard of.

This now has expanded into many classes of entries not connected with schools. A Junior Department has been added and is in the fine new metal exhibition buildings where roofs do not leak, floors are clean concrete, restrooms are adequate, modern educational exhibits are of many sorts, and chances to earn premiums are plentiful.

Time marches on and most of the changes are good—flies and mosquitoes are few. Big, new cattle, sheep, swine barns and sheds, a fine amphitheatre with reserved seating for really good evening pleasure are there.

Remember that before electricity was in common use there were no artificial lights at the fairgrounds and the day ended when the sun went down. We wondered if the man from Thomson with his load of homegrown melons at the gate would still have some left so we could buy one on the way home.

Fair Reflects Our Changing Society

The author, longtime superintendent of the floriculture and horticulture departments for the Whiteside County Fair, reviews the 1980 entries in one of the modern buildings—no more dirt floors.

Showmen present their Hereford steers for the judge at the 1963 Whiteside County Fair in Morrison.

32. Watching this Wonderful World

June 1981

This story is not about visitors who come to the house we usually write about, but is about a large brick house with many rooms. Some guests who come have planned the visit long in advance, others have not, but each is welcome and made to feel like a very special person.

Nearly every room of this big house has a picture window, the source of hours of entertainment—beautifully kept lawns in all directions; children playing safely in yards whose boundaries are flowers and shrubs, not barbed wire fences; beach gear drying on a line; swing sets; junior-size vehicles parked beside the grownups' cars and campers; rose bushes in gorgeous bloom; the early morning sun shining on the pole that next December will hold aloft the Star of Bethlehem; the big elevators assuring food for months ahead.

Bushy the Squirrel performs his breath-taking highwire on the utility wires, pausing midway between poles to test his balance—it works! When the dew is off, morning brings the ambitious young man mowing the lawn; the squirrel, some blue jays, the ever present sparrow, a pair of mourning doves grieving—or is it their "I love, love, love" song as they sit side-by-side on a wire high above the street traffic. The pair of cardinals flashing in and out of a conifer growing on some lucky family's yard; they will be the first to hear the red bird's whistling welcome to the new day.

Activity tapers off during the heat of the day, but resumes toward evening. The hard-working, drab mother robin sits atop a convenient post and encourages father robin to pull a little harder as he tugs from a neighbor's lawn inch after inch of a reckless young

Watching this Wonderful World

nightcrawler which had emerged a bit too early to begin its "night on the town." Extracted at last it becomes the final stuffing for this day for those gaping little mouths in the tree nearby.

Off to the south in the distance appears a scraggly line of crows, probably coming from a distant scavenging route to spend the night at their rookery along the river. One almost can hear the leader urging the young crows to "Shape up, back there, a nice straight line now as we approach Lyndon. They're having their 10th annual Crow Festival and we mustn't disappoint them. They are the folks who finally recognized our importance in the scheme of things."

The setting sun shines on the tall silos and metal roofs of farmsteads set in fields of shining green corn. What a wonderful country this is!

As darkness nears, the insects appear at the windows and martins swirl by in big circles scooping up mosquitoes. Is it 1,700 or 17,000 of these pests a martin consumes each day?

A night hawk on urgent business hurries past the window. A dragonfly pauses to look in. Moths circle the lights. An airplane on its regular route to the Quad Cities catches the sun's last rays and for a few seconds glows in the sky. Much later, the moon shines in—my God, How Great Thou Art, to control the cosmos and yet ensure that no baby robin goes to bed hungry!

Then morning again; if only we had watched during the night. On the neighbor's lawn we had noticed many circles of dark green grass, perhaps where tall trees once grew, were cut down, the stumps ground down and sodded over. It's well known by folks who believe in fairies that these fairy rings are the areas "little people" seek to hold their nocturnal gatherings. They bring along their ringside seats on which to rest between dances—some folks say they are just toad stools.

Those cobwebs we see now, covered with dew really are the diamond-studded scarves the fairies wore and cast aside when, like Cinderella, they overstayed the dance. The sun changes the gossamer to a cobweb and the diamonds melt into dew. Fairy rings are said to bring good fortune to folks who have them and don't frighten away the "little people."

(Editor's note: The view described is just one block north of the Lincoln Highway, from a room at the Morrison Community Hospital.)

Index

Index

Crouch
  Ashbel, **88**, 91
  Ashbel C., 86, 87
  Dwight, 87, 90
  Dwight M., 86, 87
  John A., 88
  Melvin, 90
  Melvin D., 87
  Mrs. Margaret McKee, 90
Crouch School, iv, 72, 88, 89, 90, 92, 93
Crow Festival, 117

D

Daniels
  Patricia, 85
DeKalb, IL, 93
Dierks
  Lester, 93
Downers Grove, IL, 82
Dust Bowl, 16
Dykstra
  Clarence, 90
  Jacob J., 90

E

Early
  Rev. A.M., 99
East Clinton, IL, 20, 21, 76
Edleman
  Milton, 44
Entwhistle
  Mrs. Arthur J., 98
  Wayne, 98
Erie, IL, 99, 102, 103

F

Fairchild
  Major John, 8
Farm Bureau, 75
Farmer's Elevator of Morrison, 93
Farmers' Institute, 75
Feldman

Clifford, 43
Fenton, IL, 100
Floral Hall, 108, 114
Ford, vii, 33, 77
Fort Dearborn, 4, 7, 9
Fort Leavenworth, KS, 4
Fort Yuma, AZ, 8
Foss
  Sam Walter, 30
Fourth of July, 70, 71, 83, 109
Fox and Goose, 78
Fulton, IL, iii, vi, 3, 4, 5, 23, 25, 38, 43, 55, 56, 73, 78, 87, 90, 91, 93, 94, 101, 102, 104, 111

G

Garden Plain Township, IL, 76, 98, 100, 101, 102, 104
gasohol, 58
Genesee, IL, 100, 101
Gidel
  Jerry, vi
  Susan Abbott, v, vi
Goff
  Mrs. Della Bull, 22
Goff School, 73
gold rush, 5
Goodenough
  Orville, vi, i, vi
Great Depression, iv, v, 18, 20, 24, 105
Greip
  Walter, 43
Gridley
  James G., 73
Gridley School, 73
gunsmith, 4
gypsies, 11, 12

H

Hamilton
  Henry, 14
Haring
  Earl, 43

Index

harness racing, 110
Hendricks
   B.F., 76
Henry County Hereford Association, 45
Hereford, 2, 41, 43, 45, 115
Hewitt
   J. Gordon, Jr., 86
hobos, 10
home rule, 74
homemade soap, 109
Hopkins, 104
Hopkins township, 100
Hopkins, IL, 103, 104
Household Science Club, 75
husking pegs, 47, 48

I

Illiniwek, 40, 43
Illinois Hereford Association, 45
Independence, MO, 7
Indians, i, 5, 7, 9, 22, 77
Injun Summer, 55

J

Jacobsen
   Bill, 75
Jesus, 80, 81
Jones
   Gary, 85
   Keith, 41
Jordan, IL, 100

K

Kelly
   M.R., 99
Kentland, IN, 41
kerosene lamps, 38, 74, 84
King Jr.
   Martin Luther, iv, 21

L

Lahey, 87
Lamb sawmill, 87
Landow
   Brett, vi
   Jan Abbott, v, vi
Lee Bros., 43
Lewis
   Levi, 89
Libby's Band, 112
Lincoln Highway, i, iii, iv, 9, 33, 79, 117
Little International, 43
Lockhart, IL, 76
Lyndon, IL, 100, 101, 102, 103, 104, 117

M

Martin
   John, 75
Maxfield
   Stanley, 93
McCutcheon
   John T., 55
McKee
   Arthur C., 86
   James, 87
McKray
   Warren T., 41
Mechanicsville, IA, 41
Merema
   Clarence, 93
   Kenneth, 93
   Robert, 86, 92
   Roberta, 93
   Stanley, 93
merry-go-round, v, 24, 106, 111
Meyer
   Slim, 43
Minnesota, 3
Mississippi River, iii, vi, 3, 4, 20, 72, 77, 100
Model T, 29, 36, 74, 77
Mohave tribe, 8

Index

Index

John, 41
Seely
    Col. E., 99, 100
Seifken
    Joyce, 85
Sentinel, AZ, 8
Sharer
    Dorothy, 85
Sherman, TX, 8
Short
    Amos, 72
Siefken, 22
Sikkema
    Harold, 94
silos, 50, 92, 93, 94, 117
slave, 5, 6, 8, 91
slave stick, 6
Smaltz
    Roy, 54
Smith
    Harold, 93
    Kathy, 85
    Lawana, 85
smokehouse, 34
snow, 38, 62, 78
Snyder
    Arnold, 85
    Edwin, 85
    Sandra, 85
    W.C., 87
Spring Valley Presbyterian Church, 45
Spring Valley, IL, 72
Springfield, MA, 4
St. Louis, 4
St. Paul, 4
State Line Rides, 113
Sterling, IL, 101, 102, 103, 104
Stowe
    Harriett Beecher, 4
Sunday School, 80, 81, 82

T

team, 2, 25, 43, 48, 51, 52, 54, 63, 72, 74, 88

Tervelt
    John, 85
The House by The Side of the Road, ii, 30
The Pines, vi, 13, 79
Thiem
    George, 75
toboggans, 79
tramps, 9, 10, 11, 14

U

U.S. Route 30, iii
Uncle Tom's Cabin, 4
Underground Railroad, iv, 5, 6, 92
Union Grove, IL, 20, 42, 45, 89, 95, 101, 102, 103
Unionville, IL, 72
University of Illinois, 12, 42, 43, 45, 56
Ustick Township, IL, 7, 59, 72, 86, 88, 89, 93, 104

V

Valk
    Kathleen, 85
    Timmy, 85
Vermont, 4

W

Watkins Man, 23, 24
Whiteside County Central Agricultural Society, 98
Whiteside County Fair, iv, v, 45, 98, 106, 110, 115
Wiersema
    Kenneth, 93
Wisconsin, 3
World War I, 21, 42, 61, 91
Wray
    Karen, 85

ORDER FORM

To order *House by the Side of the Road* mail a copy of this order form with a check made payable to Pines Publishing, Inc. to:

Pines Publishing, 9896 Lincoln Road, Morrison, IL 61270;

Or, order online at: www.pinespublishing.com in a secure environment using your PayPal account.

Name: _____

Address: _____

City & State: _____

Zip: _____

Phone#: _____

__ Yes, send me news and story-telling updates from Pines Publishing. My email address is: _____

Discount schedule when ordering directly from publisher:

> 1-2 books   No discount ($14.95 each)
> 3-4 books   15% discount ($12.71 each)
> 5+ books   30% discount ($10.46 each)
> *Where applicable, Illinois sales tax included*

For large quantities, contact the publisher for discount.

Please send me _____ copies of *House by the Side of the Road* at
$_____each for a total of $_____
Add $2.50 shipping for the first book $_____
Plus $0.50 for each additional book $_____
                             Total: $_____

TELL YOUR STORIES!

If you're inspired to tell stories of your life that should be preserved, send 'em on! We will consider any and all for publishing on our Web site. Send your stories by email to stories@pinespublishing.com.

Suggested topics may include:
Farm Life
Fun at the Fair
Sports Stories
Telling Tales Out of School
Praise the Lord!
What I Did On My Summer Vacation
You're In the Army, Now!
When I Was Your Age...
Kids Will Be Kids
Close Encounters With Interesting People
How I Met Your Dad
Surviving Family Gatherings
My First Car
House and Home
Pets are Family, Too
Everyday Miracles

Contact Susan at info@pinespublishing.com for information regarding publishing your own book of life stories.